Church Doors
Open Outward

Church Doors Open Outward

A PRACTICAL GUIDE TO BEGINNING COMMUNITY MINISTRY

DOROTHY B. BLOOM

Judson Press ® Valley Forge

CHURCH DOORS OPEN OUTWARD

Copyright © 1987
Judson Press, Valley Forge, PA 19482-0851

Library of Congress Cataloging-in-Publication Data

Bloom, Dorothy B.
    Church doors open outward.

    Includes bibliographical references.
    1. Church and the world. 2. Pastoral theology.
I. Title.
BR115.W6B55 1987   253   87-4216
ISBN 0-8170-1117-X

Dedicated to
my husband
who has helped me grow

Foreword

Jesus came into this world to establish his kingdom. Each of the Synoptic Gospels state that Jesus began his earthly ministry by declaring that the kingdom of God was at hand. As he preached his sermons, he outlined the principles of his kingdom, and as he told his parables, he let his audiences know that these wonderful stories were given to explain what his kingdom was all about.

The kingdom of God, which Jesus brought with him when he burst into history, was not something that was meant to be otherworldly. His kingdom, though not of this world, was certainly planned to be in this world. Jesus taught his disciples to pray, "Thy kingdom come, They will be done, *on earth* as it is in heaven."

It was Christ's intention to transform this world into the kind of world that he willed for it to be in the first place. That is why he was crucified. A man does not get spiked to a cross because he tells people to be loving; he gets to speak at Rotary meetings.

Jesus came not only to transform the subjective emotions of people so that they would be loving, but also to initiate a new social order that would be permeated with his justice. Those who had a vested interest in maintaining the old unjust order knew this and laid plans to destroy him. Those who grasped the fact that their positions of wealth, power, and prestige were dependent on the continuation of the societal *status quo* recognized Jesus as a threat.

The Jews in Jesus' day had a clear idea about what their messiah would do when he came to walk among them. When they greeted one another or bade one another farewell, they would always do it with the word *shalom*. For them, shalom meant much more than its rough translation, "peace," implies. For them, shalom meant the establishing of Jehovah's kingdom on earth and the emergence of Israel as the divine vehicle through which God's rule would be extended to include all the nations of the world. The Jews believed that this kingdom, signified by the word shalom, would be a society in which the hungry would be fed, the unjust custodians of power brought down, and the lowly lifted up. They believed that when shalom was manifested in the kingdom of God, justice would roll down upon all people, and the poor and the oppressed would have "good news" for a change.

In the midst of the American fundamentalist/liberal controversy, the message of the kingdom of God was often discarded by evangelical Christians because we considered crusades for a better world to be part of the liberal agenda. We evangelicals committed ourselves enthusiastically to personal evangelism, a task that we perceived to be sorely neglected by our theologically liberal adversaries. We thought that a church committed to social justice might not be a church with much of a commitment to winning individuals to Christ.

That dialectic tension between the evangelicals and the liberals is still evident in America. But over the last couple of decades, we evangelicals have begun to overcome some of the fears and anxieties that earlier had troubled us. We have grown in number and become a major force for social change. With our newfound strength and self-assurance, we are increasingly open to dialogue with our liberal friends.

Today, evangelicals are increasingly promoting a wholistic gospel that incorporates a concern for social justice with our deep concern for individual salvation. We have come to realize that part of the purpose of God's saving work is to change us all into persons who can work for kingdom goals. Now it remains for our liberal friends to realize the importance that we have placed on personal evangelism. It is important for them to recognize that without personal evangelism, there will be few recruits to participate in God's revolution in history.

In this book, Dorothy Bloom sets forth a balance that *all* Christians can embrace. Her strong evangelical theology that teaches that the work of the kingdom begins with Bible study in local churches should draw loud "amens" from evangelicals. Her passionate concern for social justice should be a welcome balm to those who share the liberal's agony for the oppressed of the world.

This book covers a whole range of social concerns. From American foreign policy to the sufferings of the elderly, Dorothy Bloom carefully examines the Biblical basis for making judgments on social issues and prescribes ways for ordinary church people to take corrective action. We people in the pews have had a need for such a book as this for a long time, and I, for one, am glad it is here.

Dorothy Bloom demonstrates that ordinary persons who allow God to transform them through the power of the Holy Spirit and are willing to be instructed by the Word of God can make a difference in their world. While the kingdom of God will not come in its fullness until the return of Christ, books like this one can, in the meantime, encourage us to be the kind of leaven that initiates those changes that point to the kingdom already at hand.

Dr. Anthony Campolo
Eastern College
St. Davids, PA

Contents

A Personal Testimony

Kay's spirit of unselfishness comes from parents who spent much of their time helping those less fortunate than they were. She had a retarded younger sister and this relationship taught Kay the importance of accepting the person behind the outward appearance.

When Kay became a Christian, her church taught her the importance of serving others; but her service always seemed to be within the four walls of the church building. She had boundless energy, so that even with a large family she was able to devote a great deal of time to church work.

One day at the supermarket she met a neighbor, a young woman, who said to her, "I have been meaning to call you but you are always so busy with your church work!" Later, reflecting on her neighbor's remark, Kay realized she was so involved with her church that she had no time to be a friend to her neighbors.

Does Kay's experience seem familiar? Think back to a time when you first became aware of someone else's needs. How did you react?

A pastor of a young growing church in the Midwest recalls making a pastoral call on a woman who had been coming to morning worship for several months. When no one answered his knock on the front door, although he could hear sounds of activity within, he went to the back door. The woman welcomed him into the house. As they walked through the kitchen, the pastor saw in a large crib a young lad of about 12 years of age. When they had sat down in the living room, the woman said, "That's Eddy. He has the mentality of a baby of six months." The pastor later reflected that he could preach all year, but not until he went into that home could he really minister to that woman.

As a layperson, I became aware that God was calling me to look at the needs of people in my community troubled with a variety of problems. In studying my Bible more carefully, I discovered that I'd missed a major theme in the Scriptures, namely, that God has a special concern for the world's poor and oppressed—and that God calls us to share that burden. As I discovered community needs, I wondered why my church and other churches seemed so removed from the real pain of the world.

The First Baptist Church, Scottsdale, Arizona, where I am a member, has a magnificent sanctuary whose outstanding feature is a large stained-glass skylight rising like a lantern some seventy or eighty feet into the air from the middle of the ceiling. The light within can be seen for blocks. The architects had personally experienced the congregation's warmth of fellowship and worship and designed the "lantern" to symbolize the inner Spirit shining out on a dark world. They wanted it to say that the church was a light which "cannot be hid" (Matthew 5:14).

Some churches are beginning to have that same insight. They are discovering in their communities persons who almost literally are crying out for attention. God has called us to minister and witness in the world. Perhaps yours is a church where much energy is focused on individuals and programs within the church. This book can help you "hear" and "see" your neighbors who are asking for a sign that can "show them something of the character of God," as William Barclay puts it.[1] Today Christians are needed to be the presence of God in servant roles in their communities.

The Sunday bulletins of many churches indicate a great deal of activity going on within the buildings, meetings for this and that. It is as though the doors of the church only swing *inward* so people can come *into* the building. There appear to be no structured ways for church members to go out into the community to witness and bring healing to persons not yet ready to become part of the organized church.

My personal journey toward community awareness began with a feeling of dissatisfaction. I felt as if my Christian life was on hold, waiting for something to happen. I did not share these feelings with anyone, maybe because I did not know exactly what was wrong. Then I began to take part in a personal enrichment group that met once a week. Slowly my world expanded as I seriously considered what God wanted of me when the command was given to us— including me—to "go into all the world." Problems of people outside my church began to penetrate my consciousness.

Three friends and I decided to meet regularly to discuss the needs of children in our community and to find out what needs were not already being met. We began to see the community through new eyes—and we discovered it had a complexity of needs. This led each of us into different arenas of service as we sought to answer God's call to ministry.

By deliberately choosing to become aware of the world around me, I discovered some new things about myself. I discovered fears I had never admitted before. I also found I had talents I did not know existed. I began accepting responsibility for myself. I opened my ears to the world around me to hear the cries of pain and loneliness and to feel empathy for troubled men and women.

I was helped by a number of Christians who had already stepped outside the church doors to live and work with others in the world. They taught me that the way to begin community ministry was to look at how the Master himself related to others. Jesus saw people where they were, with their needs and longings, and accepted them as they were. He ministered to the whole person. Jesus, with Spirit-opened eyes, "saw a man called Matthew sitting at the tax office; and he said to him, 'Follow me.' And he rose and followed him" (Matthew 9:9). Jesus saw more than a man at a tax desk. He saw a total person, saw his potential and his longing to be whole. Because the Master always looked through eyes that were open fully, he saw a man others might overlook, even despise.

As I sought to find answers for my life, I became aware of God's leading. While attending graduate school, I experienced a divine call to help churches discover community needs that they could meet. I received a grant from the Board of National Ministries of the American Baptist Churches, U.S.A., for the purpose of assisting churches in the Phoenix area to look at needs in their community ministry and meet those needs by practicing biblical principles.

This book, *Church Doors Open Outward*, is a follow-up to that project. It is written to help others develop a ministry of healing in their communities through the hope and love of Jesus Christ. Each chapter is divided into two sections, the first dealing with the theory behind the process of beginning community ministry, and the second providing specific activities with which to begin the process.

Chapter 1 begins with Bible study, in which we discover some of the passages in which God is telling us to minister to the needy and oppressed. In Chapter 2 we study a few of the problems in society which call out for tangible expressions of our concern. Our understanding of the needs becomes more personal in Chapter 3 as we study our own local community to find specific situations where our ministry might begin. Then, in Chapter 4, we deal with the strategy of getting our own church congregation interested in participating with us in community action. Finally, in Chapter 5, we consider how to firm up a program and put it into action.

I have written this book in the hope that at least a few persons in your church will join in groups to study the Bible and the community and respond by taking leadership in the kind of social ministry that is described here. I realize that this may be a lonely effort in some churches, but I urge you—even if you yourself are the only one who responds—to go ahead with it. Although this book is designed for groups, it recognizes that individuals may use it also. Therefore at certain points alternative approaches are suggested for those who must "go it alone." With a little imagination it will not be difficult to make other adaptations.

The book has been written to provide a process for moving into the community to do the ministry God has given us. It also chronicles a journey that begins when we experience God's saving and transforming power in our lives. It continues as we become whole in Christ and are set free to see others with a new understanding. Our journey will lead us to become more aware of the world's need for the message of hope and love that only Jesus Christ can give. As we respond to God's call to ministry and become servants within our community the light of God's love can then shine out from our churches as cities that "cannot be hid."

—Dorothy B. Bloom

—————————— **1** ——————————

Starting with the Bible

> "Go to this people, and say,
> You shall indeed hear but never understand,
> and you shall indeed see but never perceive.
> For this people's heart has grown dull,
> and their ears are heavy of hearing,
> and their eyes they have closed;
> lest they should perceive with their eyes,
> and hear with their ears,
> and understand with their heart,
> and turn for me to heal them."
> —Acts 28:26–27

What does God expect his church to do in our world today? Most of us would agree that it should change people—that it should help them to become more fully the kind of creatures he destined them to become. We do not all agree so easily, however, as to whether we are expected to change people as individuals or as a society—or both.

The issue hinges on two concepts of the kingdom of God which Jesus proclaimed. On the one hand he spoke of a future kingdom in which his people would be rewarded and fulfilled. On the other hand he declared that the kingdom was already present. The former concept deals with life after death, the latter with life upon this earth. Many people have interpreted the future emphasis in terms of personal salvation in the kingdom which is to come after their death. Others have seen the contemporary emphasis as validation of a social gospel which seeks the perfection of a kingdom already present.

If the church must choose between these two concepts, then its options are located in two entirely differing forms of ministry. If it chooses to think of the kingdom as only in the future, it will stress personal evangelism and the devotional life. If it prefers to think of the kingdom as already present, it will plunge into social action, in order that the values of the present kingdom may be maximized. Many churches have chosen one route or the other, becoming either highly evangelistic in their stress on personal conversion and piety or vigorously activist in their pursuit of social change. Whichever direction they choose, they risk neglecting the other.

But must the church choose? Is not the situation "both/and" instead of "either/or"? Jesus did not exclude either concept. He spoke approvingly of both, often in different situations. Let us turn to the Bible for clarification.

The Present Kingdom and the Social Gospel

Before the coming of Christ our Bible consisted only of the Old Testament, and this had many passages pointing to fulfillment of the kingdom in the future. Prophetic books like Isaiah abound in these references. With the coming of John the Baptist, however, a new message was proclaimed: "Repent, for the kingdom of heaven is at hand" (Matthew 3:2). Fulfilling this announcement after his baptism by John, Jesus declared again and again that the kingdom had arrived (for instance, Matthew 4:17), and furthermore he instructed his disciples to deliver the same message. Jesus went on to heal people and even to cast out demons, pointing to these acts as proof that the kingdom had come (Luke 11:20).

This arrival of the kingdom of God proclaims a restoration of the relationship between God and the human race. We see Jesus' life revealed as a demonstration of the essence of the kingdom (John 6:38)—a life bringing harmony of body, mind, and spirit. Jesus preached that the kingdom is precious because it has saving power. It will drive back the forces of Satan. Even though it is temporal, it is here now. It has begun.[2]

Involved in this interpretation is a movement called the Social Gospel, which originated more than a hundred years ago, affirming the presence of God in the world. Christians who stressed the Social Gospel believed that God's call was to join the kingdom, to serve others, and to serve as models for Christian life in the world. Even before the term "Social Gospel" was invented, however, Christians had been expressing their faith through such causes as the temperance and antislavery movements. In this new movement they became concerned about child labor, housing, disease control, slum conditions, women's rights, regulation of public utilities, and many other social problems. Through Christian action they sought to transform social structures and institutions so that these would embody Christian principles, thereby bringing about a more compassionate and sensitive world.

The Future Kingdom and Personal Salvation

Jesus also taught that the kingdom was coming, a future event. In his parables of the mustard seed and the leaven in a loaf of bread he taught that the present small beginnings can lead to glorious fulfillment. He also spoke of a future kingdom when he said that some of his disciples would not die before they saw him coming in his glory—by which he meant his kingdom (Matthew 16:28).[3]

Many Christians over the centuries have felt that this accent on future fulfillment is underscored by the familiar "Great Commission" passage, Matthew 28:18–20, in which Jesus calls his followers to proclaim the gospel throughout the world. They have therefore seen their task of evangelism as bringing individuals to accept Christ immediately in this world, looking toward their acceptance into the future kingdom of God. Such evangelism is expected to lead to personal transformation which, in turn, will result in a more sensitive and compassionate world.

The Kingdom Present and Future

Do these two systems of belief seem contradictory to you? They do to many people, but they do not need to be. As David Moberg puts it, "It is only as persons are born again by the Holy Spirit that they become spiritual children of God, but the gospel of Jesus Christ has far-reaching social implications."[4]

We need to accept these two views of the kingdom of God—both of them, not just one—in order to grasp how the Christian is to respond to God's call. Because of Jesus, the kingdom has come. Jesus asks us to join with him to preach the kingdom of God in the present tense. Thus we testify to his saving grace to all who believe, and we bring healing and hope to others by ministering in love. At the same time we proclaim that the kingdom is still to come. As we say in the Lord's Prayer, we look toward fulfillment "on earth as it is in heaven" (Matthew 6:10). Our own efforts will not in themselves bring the kingdom to completion, but we can bear witness to the coming, by God's grace, of a kingdom in which all will be made new.

Reconciling the Paradox

Paradoxical as it may seem to link these two seemingly conflicting views of the kingdom, this linkage is exactly what we find in the Bible. We must find ways to relate the two to each other in our own experience. We can do so in various ways—for instance by testifying verbally to God's redeeming love, even while performing acts of loving kindness toward other individuals and while working with others in social action to bring about a more just world. We cannot say that any one of these methods excludes the others. In fact, we may well say instead that the methods go hand in hand. "The Lord is just in all his ways, and kind in all his doings" (Psalm 145:17).

A couple of examples illustrate churches that took to heart this concept of a ministry that testifies through action as well as words. One congregation developed a Boy Scout troop for youth with special learning needs. As the church provided them with an atmosphere of acceptance and self-worth, young scouts began to catch the vision of God and his love for them. Another church decided to minister to persons detained in a nearby prison as illegal aliens, and in the process discovered that there was need for prison reforms. This church's role thus became twofold: to preach the Good News of Jesus Christ and to bring hope by changing an institution.

Values and Beliefs

Even while we are reading the Bible, our understanding of it is shaped by our values, and conversely our values are shaped by our understanding of the Bible. During the great revivals of earlier years, the dominant theme of evangelical preachers regarding social issues was one that recognized sin to be corporate as well as personal. They preached that sin has its roots not only in individuals but in society as a whole. Their concern for the sins of society led them to work for reform of evils within their community. As Moberg puts it,

"Evangelical Christianity was a major influence on many social reforms in industrial societies during the eighteenth and nineteenth centuries. It had a profound impact upon the abolition movement, prison reform, the treatment of the mentally ill, and working conditions of industrial laborers. . . ."[5]

Our values are based on our trust in certain intrinsic beliefs. Among the important values to consider, as cited by Robert M. Moroney, are personal freedom, equality, and community, but these sometimes contradict each other, as he has pointed out: "While all three may be desirable . . . they cannot all be maximized at once. In fact, more of one will inevitably result in less of the others." Let us look at these three values and add a fourth: justice.

Personal Freedom

As Christians we accept the value of personal freedom because we know it through individual experience with God through Jesus Christ. Jesus told his critics that he had the authority to forgive personal sins (Mark 2:5). The apostle Paul wrote that we are called to the kingdom as individuals (1 Thessalonians 2:12). He has also reminded us that we are called to freedom in order to serve others (Galatians 5:13). We cannot accept our freedom lightly, nor may we abuse it by thinking only of ourselves.

As we claim forgiveness for our personal sins, we acknowledge that we also share in the corporate sin of our community and society. God makes us aware of such sins. "Come now, and let us reason together, says the Lord, though your sins are like scarlet, they shall be as white as snow; though they are red like crimson, they will become like wool" (Isaiah 1:18). We need to be reminded that we cannot simply read this verse as it relates to our individual sin and our need for personal salvation. It was written by Isaiah, speaking of God's action toward the sinful people of Israel. It referred to their corporate sin and their corporate salvation. As for us, we can live out our thankfulness for this promise by living as God's redeemed people in our community.

Equality

An emphasis on equality will accentuate the need for an egalitarian society that seeks justice and a reduction in age-old inequities. Jesus was a believer in equality. He saw people as people. Whether it was a person of another ethnic group such as the good Samaritan (Luke 10:29–37), one of another sex such as the woman at the well (John 4:7–26), or one of another social class such as Matthew the tax collector (Matthew 9:9–13), he saw the individual only as a human being and a child of God. Everyone needed God's love and forgiveness; everyone needed the compassion of fellow human beings.

Community

Christian people are strengthened by fellowship with other Christian people. They need community. As Albert Rasmussen has put it, "We now know that the basic biblical Gospel is both intensely personal in its call to the new life and that, at the same time, it calls men into a life of Christian fellowship and responsibility in all of their relationships."[7]

The Old Testament tells us that God established a divine covenant with Abraham's descendants, the community known as Israel (Genesis 12:1–3). In the New Testament we discover a new covenant with the new community of believers, the Christian church (Luke 22:20). Both covenant communities have been intensely meaningful. For Israel, the exodus from Egypt brought freedom from oppression to all its members. For the church the common experience of salvation through Jesus Christ brought a sharing of strength, joy, and purpose.

The church has much in common with Israel. Many of God's commandments given in those early years of the Old Testament before the coming of Christ are still as valid as they ever were and help to bind us together as a church. Beyond these, as Christians we have a common covenant with God, a common goal of witnessing to salvation in Christ, and a common responsibility for ministering to persons in need. It is through this community, as well as through individuals, that God shines into a dark world. It is to the church that Jesus gave the message to go and make disciples of all nations (Matthew 28:18–20). Sometimes we wonder how we can go so far away from our homes to carry out this mission, and perhaps we cannot do so. Nevertheless we can respond to God's call by ministering in our own community.

Justice

As we try to balance the concerns of the individual and the community, we cannot forget the need for justice that God commands throughout Scripture. We read of it in Deuteronomy 16:20, "Justice, and only justice, you shall follow, that you may live and inherit the land which the Lord your God gives you." Even more eloquently a great prophet speaks to us, "But let justice roll down like waters, and righteousness like an everflowing stream" (Amos 5:24).

Justice must be a way of life (Leviticus 19:15). God uses the standards of justice to show us righteousness (Matthew 25:34–40). The psalmist sings praises to the Lord, whose word is upright and who loves righteousness and justice (Psalm 33:4–5). As we draw closer to God in worship, we begin to see the world through God's eyes. We discover God's concern for the world's oppressed. We understand that righteousness is always joined to justice.

In Short —

Our witness is based on our faith as we understand the message of God's kingdom. Jesus came into the world as our God-given Savior, bringing salvation through his atoning death on the cross. Thus the kingdom of God has broken forth upon the world! Never again shall the world remain in darkness. The resurrection points to the day when the kingdom is complete and Christ becomes Lord of the whole earth. His followers have a message to proclaim to the world, both individual and corporate, a message that the reign of God has already begun and yet is to come fully in the future. We are called both to preach and to transform. As Birch and Rasmussen have worded it, "When the church does what it is supposed to do, *as church*, it transforms not only the lives of its members, but the life of their culture as well."[8] In so doing we respond to the biblical concerns for freedom, equality, community, and justice.

Activities—
Finding Insights in the Bible

To discover what God says about our world and how we as Christians may respond, it will be a helpful experience to form one or more Bible study groups (perhaps as small as two or three persons and certainly no larger than ten or twelve). Although groups have a value that is not available to individuals, don't be discouraged if you are unable to form one. Do the work by yourself, but gain some of the value of a group by asking a friend to pray for you.

The material which follows suggests four areas of study, to be done in four separate sessions:

Activity 1 examines passages that deal with love and sharing.

Activity 2 examines the message and actions of Jesus in light of his statement about his ministry. try.

Activity 3 examines the parable of the good Samaritan to discover the meaning of community ministry.

Activity 4 examines what the Bible has to say about justice.

Each study includes suggestions for biblical material, as well as background information, ideas for discussion or meditation, assignments for individual work, and an opportunity for group sharing.

(Note: Although the guidance material which follows is worded in term of group use, you can easily adapt it to individual study if you elect to do so. At some points suggestions for such adaptation are inserted as examples).

It is important for the pastor to share in this project. If it is being initiated by a lay person, he or she should meet with the pastor to enlist support, and the pastor should be kept informed as to the group's activities. Insofar as possible, the support of the entire congregation should be sought, and the pas-

tor can help with this effort. Do not be discouraged, however, if the congregation or even the pastor should prove to be less supportive than you might wish. Enormous power is available when at least two or three persons come together to seek guidance and then act on the leading of the Holy Spirit.

Some Suggestions for Effective Groups

1. Bring together a number of persons who are interested in discovering God's will for community ministry and willing to covenant with each other to meet for a specific number of sessions (perhaps four).

2. Select a person to lead the first session. This individual can continue as leader for subsequent sessions, or the responsibility can be passed around, as the group prefers.

3. Ask for agreement that everybody will study the Bible passages, accept and work on assignments, and share personal discoveries and feelings openly with each other.

4. It will be helpful for members to keep personal journals containing their thoughts, feelings, new ideas, and opinions. These may be shared with the group or with others in the church at a later date.

5. Keep the group task-oriented, with its purpose constantly in mind: that the members—and the church as a whole, insofar as possible—should become involved as deeply as possible in community ministry.

Activity 1: Responding to God's Messages of Love and Caring

Getting Started

Get acquainted with other members of the group.

Share your concerns regarding church experiences in community ministry. Be positive; emphasize the good things. This must not degenerate into a gripe session about what the church is or is not doing.

Use a chalkboard or newsprint to state the topic, "Responding to God's Messages of Love and Caring." (If you are studying individually, begin your journal with these words, and add your personal responses as you think of them.)

Bible Study

Introduce the Bible passages in this study by inviting the group to read them and relate them to their own experiences. Show how a Christian is called upon to associate his or her faith with others in a social relationship.

Luke 10:25–28

1. How are love for God and love for neighbor intertwined?
2. How did Jesus demonstrate love to persons around him?
3. Take a close look at verse 28. What did Jesus mean by the word "live"?
4. Share (or write down) an experience you have had in loving a neighbor.

1 John 4:20–21

1. Share with the group (or record in your own journal) a time when you felt you had a direct message from God. What made you sure about it?
2. How can you apply the message in these verses to your life?

Matthew 5:43–48

1. Who comes to your mind when you think of an enemy?
2. Did you think of someone
—who might physically harm you?
—who has maligned you?
—who says hurtful things to you (especially a relative or close friend)
—who has a different set of beliefs from yours?

Micah 6:8

1. What are some specific ways by which you try to live out this verse in your daily life?
2. How do you relate this verse to involvement in ministry *with* and *to* your community?

Invite the group to comment on these statements:

1. Love is social. It can be a relationship between God and individuals or between persons.

> The gospel is eminently personal, for each man has his own encounter with God and chooses to accept or reject Him. But the gospel also is social, for every person is deeply enmeshed in a social situation, and it is impossible to love God while hating one's neighbor.
>
> —David H. Moberg

2. Sometimes it is easier to accept the gospel message intellectually than to activate it in our lives. "The essence of the gospel is not ethics, yet . . . the gospel has profound ethical implications," says Moberg.[10]

Case Study: The Flooded Town

Homes in one section of your town have been flooded out several times in the past few years. This spring there has been another period of very heavy rain. The river has risen drastically above flood level and many homes have water as much as three feet deep in their living rooms. Three kinds of responses which might be made to such a crisis could be identified as social concern, social welfare, and social action:

Social concern is a kind of caring which expresses itself in a spontaneous outpouring or a planned approach to help persons meet basic human needs such as food, clothing, shelter, and medicine.

Social welfare is a program to alleviate the social problems of men, women, and children, generally through some form of government action.

Social action is an organized effort through political or other processes to reform the basic conditions that cause a social problem.

With these definitions in mind, how might you respond to the flood situation in terms of each of these three approaches?

Assignment

The leader should duplicate and distribute Handout 1 with these instructions: "Prior to our next study session, read Handout 1. Think through your answers to the questions in the second paragraph. Be prepared to share them with the group." (If you are working individually, study the material yourself and share your thoughts with a friend or pastor.)

HANDOUT 1

Read Exodus 3:1–10.

Imagine yourself at your own burning bush. Think about your world, your neighborhood concerns, your workplace, the places where you do business, your involvement in local, state, and national government (either just as a voter or in some more prominent way). Where do you see social evil at work, pervading and perverting, struggling to outdo the forces of good? Where does God see suffering and bondage? Put yourself in Moses' place at the burning bush—but in today's world. What evil might God call upon you to address? It might not be of grandiose proportions, though it could be.

What might you be commissioned to do if you were to meet God today at a burning bush?

Activity 2: Analyzing Jesus' Own Statement About His Ministry

Getting Started

Begin by sharing (or writing down) thoughts about burning-bush experiences and insights from the Activity 1 assignment.

Bible Study

Have someone read Luke 4:18–19. Ask: "What do these verses reveal about the gospel Jesus had come to preach?" Think through the meaning of what he said. Discuss the questions following each quoted phrase in the following material. (If your group is large, divide into subgroups and assign one or more of the phrases to each.)

". . . preach good news to the poor."

1. Who do you think were the poor in this verse? You might find it interesting to compare it with Matthew 5:3 and Luke 6:20.

2. Do we distort Jesus' message when we substitute the spiritually poor for those who suffer economic poverty?

3. What might we do differently if we ministered both to the poor in spirit and to those who are poor in material possessions?

". . . proclaim release to the captives. . . ."

1. Who were the captives to whom Jesus (and Isaiah) referred?

2. What does liberation mean to you?

3. To what, or whom, were Jesus' listeners (that is, the people in the synagogue) captive?

4. If Jesus came to your community and asked you to identify some captives, who would they be?

5. Have you ever visited someone in jail? Describe your experience. How did it feel when the doors clanged behind you?

". . . recovering of sight to the blind. . . ."

1. What is our ministry to the blind and other disabled persons?

2. What other kinds of blindness are there besides the physical? Could they affect you and me? How does Christ speak to this condition?

". . . set at liberty those who are oppressed. . . ."

1. Another word for "oppressed" might be "downtrodden." Can you identify some of today's oppressed or downtrodden people? Think of other countries and our own as well.

2. What is meant by setting them free?

3. How can we become involved in the liberation process?

Thinking It Through

Here are some thoughts you might want to suggest to the group for discussion and meditation:

1. Jesus declared plainly that his ministry was to overcome evil. History reveals that evil can be perpetuated by people who are highly moral in their

personal relationships. Esther Bruland and Steven Mott have said: "On a larger level, loving actions may be taking place within an evil society—as when, in a slave society, slave owners treat their slaves with kindness and generosity."[11]

2. We can sin by group action as well as by personal behavior. For example, products banned as unsafe in our nation are frequently sold by our manufacturers in other countries. Even though we may not approve of such practices, we share in the guilt because we are citizens of a democracy that does not prevent them. Evil can thus be reinforced through neglect as well as through action. Many times we fail to speak out or to act when we become aware of injustice, thereby becoming active participants in a sinful society. Such sins of omission have familiar and ugly names like discrimination, ignorance, and apathy.

3. Recalling Jesus' identification of needy groups in society in Luke 4:18–19 (the poor, the blind, the captives, the oppressed), can we think of specific groups in our own community who would fall into these categories—vulnerable groups who need the loving care of others?

4. Jesus' ministry of obedience to God was costly to him. Consider the following verses:

Luke 9:58 . . . . Cost: poverty
Philippians 2:6–8 . . . . . . Cost: humiliation
Hebrews 2:17–18 . . . . . . Cost: temptation
Hebrews 5:8 . . . . Cost: suffering
Luke 23:33 . . . . Cost: crucifixion

Jesus accepted and paid all these costs. We sometimes act as though we believe his ministry failed, as though the things he preached did not work, but we are wrong. Easter—the resurrection—is God's affirmation of Jesus' life and message. Resurrection exclaims, "It does work!" We celebrate Easter each year and remind ourselves that his gospel works. We *can* risk being disciples. Discipleship can be costly for us, as it was for him, but in the resurrection we have faith and hope.

The picture of the Servant does not end in tragedy; it ends in triumph, in vindication by God and in recognition by men. Without a doubt Jesus saw life beyond death, and the crown beyond the cross, and the glory beyond the shame, and the triumph beyond the tragedy, and the enthronement beyond the rejection.

—William Barclay

Assignment

1. Find a private place during the week and meditate on the following Scripture passages about being Jesus' disciples:

John 8:12 and 8:31
John 12:26
Ephesians 5:1–2
1 John 2:6

2. Record your insights and feelings.

3. Prepare to share these with the group, or with your pastor or some other friend.

Activity 3: Finding New Meanings for Community Ministry in the Parable of the Good Samaritan

Getting Started

If you are leading a group, give the members a few minutes to share thoughts that have come to them from the Activity 2 assignment.

Bible Study

Have someone read Luke 10:25–37.

Discuss (or meditate upon) the parable of the good Samaritan. The following quotation will help to interpret it:

Jewish devotion taught that there were 613 commandments, 365 of them negative and 248 positive, but underlying them all was a fundamental attitude, [by] which if one grasped, all the commandments would logically fall into place.

—Hillyer Straton[13]

The lawyer in this parable knew the Scriptures, but he simply did not apply them. Jesus therefore told the story to help him understand the basic attitude necessary to begin living out the truth of the commandments.

For most of us the question is the same as that of the ancient lawyer: "Who is my neighbor?" Like him, we find our answer in the parable. Let us look at the story, therefore, in terms of its principal characters: the victim, the robbers, the priest, the Levite, the Samaritan, and the innkeeper. What do we know about them? Dr. Straton's comments will help us.

The victim. He is unknown. His name is not given. He simply represents Anyone, male or female. Straton says: "He is simply 'a certain man,' by implication a Jew, a man who unquestionably represents universal humanity."[14] Have you or anyone you know ever been a victim of a robbery? Discuss or record your experiences, recollections, feelings.

The robbers. They do not appear to be unique. Robbers frequently attacked travelers on this highway. The event certainly would not have made news headlines on that day. Today there are certain areas in our country where travel is more dangerous than others. What fears do you have when you travel?

The priest. It is generally assumed that he was coming from Jerusalem, perhaps from serving in the Temple.

> The story implies that he had completed serving his course in the Temple. All of his worship was designed to carry him through the week in an attitude of praise and gratitude. But, you see, he left God in the Temple when he should have taken Him on the journey back to his home. . . ."[15]

Do you think the callousness of the priest surprised those who heard Jesus tell this story? How do we react to callousness today, especially to callousness on the part of those whose faith would seem to point them in a different direction?

The Levite. Priests were descendants of Aaron and were the only ones who could serve in the tabernacle. Levites helped the priests and instructed in the Law. The Levite in the story, like the priest, was part of the religious establishment. He studied the Scriptures. He knew the Law. Why do you think his studies had not prepared him for the highway encounter with the robbery victim? Like the lawyer who was questioning Jesus, both the priest and the Levite knew how to worship God. They both knew the Scriptures, but they had not discovered the meaning for themselves. They had not translated the truths of Scripture into their style of life. "Perhaps he was going *up* to the Temple and did not want to be delayed in the service of God, while all the time here was God's service shouting to be recognized."

With this parable in mind, what are some of the ways in which we fall short of putting our Christian beliefs into action? Narrow your answer down to specific actions or behaviors.

The Samaritan. He, too, may have gone to Jerusalem, but not to worship at the Temple. Samaritans were despised by the Jews, even considered by some to be enemies. The Samaritan, a half-breed, held different beliefs from the Jews. His forefathers, separated from the Jerusalem Jews when the Northern Kingdom's capital city was captured by the Assyrians in 721 B.C., had intermarried with non-Jews. Whenever Samaritans crossed the border into Judea, therefore, they were met with hatred and suspicion. Consider these questions:

1. Why was the Samaritan kind to the man by the side of the road? Is it likely that there was something special about him as a person? Dr. Straton guesses that there was: "For the Samaritan there was no chance about his compassion, for he had been neighborly all his life."

2. If one's lifestyle determines how a person reacts in an emergency, how can we prepare to react always in a Christian way?

The Innkeeper. We know nothing about him, not even whether he followed the Samaritan's instructions or not. Nor do we know whether the robbery victim recovered or whether the Samaritan was ever thanked. We hope for the best.

This parable is a strong reminder that as Christians we are to help people who are in trouble. Spend a few minutes, therefore, with the group in sharing experiences of spontaneously helping people—or perhaps of being so helped. Who is *our* neighbor? Is this not a question we must examine for ourselves, again and again?

> We must recognize our neighbor. The neighbor is anyone who has need, no matter what his race, creed, color, or distance from us. We must give him what *aid we can*. We cannot carry the weight or hunger of all the world, but we can use the oil and wine that *we* have.

Jesus completed this parable by saying, "Go and do likewise." It takes more than worship and knowledge of Scripture to prepare us to meet the challenges of faith. Accepting God's message and becoming a follower requires daily commitment and practice. It requires an attitude of acceptance, of not drawing lines, of showing love and care to those whose paths cross ours. It means reaching out to those in need instead of waiting for them to come to us. We must be willing to meet immediate needs; but, more than that, we must work to bring about change, to sacrifice, and to forget about the costs to ourselves.

Putting It Together

1. Using chalkboard or newsprint, list ways in which your church has been a good neighbor (or write them in your journal). Recall some of the costs in terms of time, money, and personal involvement of people. Interview some longtime members. Your church may have much more of a "good neighbor" history than the present generation of members knows. It may have been more active in the past than it is now.

2. Out of this exercise might grow a project of writing a history of the church's involvement in community ministry. This could be shared profitably with the entire congregation.

Assignment

List (or record in your journal) deeds of kindness you perform between this session and the next. Note whether they are cases of others reaching out to you or of your becoming aware of someone's need. Be prepared to share these accounts with the group, or with the pastor or some friend.

Activity 4: Studying Biblical Views of Justice

Getting Started

Follow up on the previous assignment by sharing with one another some of the acts of kindness that have been recorded since the last group session.

Bible Study

Read the following Scripture passages (in small groups, if appropriate):

Deuteronomy 32:4

Psalm 33:5
Proverbs 21:3

Each group should list the words that stand out in these passages and discuss them. Note especially the word "justice," and work out a definition of it.

Bring the small groups together and have them report their definitions, writing them on chalkboard or newsprint. Refine the several definitions into one on which the entire group agrees. You might invite a lawyer to meet with you to express his or her views on justice. Ask your visitor's opinion of your definition. How do present-day ideas of justice compare with those found in the Bible?

Consider the following distinction. What do you think of it?

Paul Ramsey, in *Basic Christian Ethics*, defines love as "regarding the good of any other individual as more than your own when he and you alone are involved" and justice as "what Christian love does when it is confronted by two or more neighbors."[19]

Use a concordance to find additional Scriptures that refer to justice, the great theme that runs throughout the Old Testament.

Consider also the following:

Amos 5:24. How do you relate *your* worship of God to acts of justice and righteousness? What are other actions you might take if you had the courage, the time, or the knowledge?

Mark 2:23–28. What does Jesus say here about justice? Even though the word does not appear in this passage, the concept is very much present. In what ways do we sometimes put our traditions, our customs, or our laws above our consideration for people?

John 8:3–11. In this episode from the life of Jesus, what do you think about his administration of mercy and justice? Can you think of any other examples in which he balanced these two values? Can you cite examples of how some of our laws provide this balance, or fail to do so? What are some ways your church demonstrates justice mixed with mercy?

These Scriptures teach us that God calls us to be just in our actions with one another in a loving and caring manner. As we read, we see how often justice is coupled with righteousness and love. Justice alone is not enough; it can be too easily distorted. We need to be led by love, grace, and mercy as we strive to turn away from injustice and toward justice.

Social problems so often are problems of social justice. Through the Scriptures, of course, we are directed to be just toward others as individuals. Beyond this, however, we are to promote systems that provide justice and to work for change in systems that are unjust. As Christians we must not despair or believe that our efforts are useless. Our hope is built on Jesus Christ, our firm foundation.

Assignment

Make copies of the following handout and distribute them to members of the group. Ask them to follow the instructions and report on it next week.

HANDOUT 2

Please meditate upon this statement during the week and write down in your journal how you would respond to the challenge it contains. At our next meeting be prepared to discuss how we can bring the challenge to our church as a whole.

Obedience to Christ demands change, the world becomes his world, the poor, the weak and the suffering are men, women and children created in his image; injustice is an affront to his creation; despair, indifference and aimlessness are replaced by hope, responsibility and purpose; and above all selfishness is transformed to love.

—Robert G. Clouse[20]

2

A World Out There That Needs Us

They were sharecroppers. For years they had dreamed of leaving this place and moving on to a home of their own. Each year they had worked and saved to make their dream come true, and today was the day. Loading their wagon, they started their journey. A rickety old bridge across a deep chasm stood between them and their destination. They held their breath all the way across. When they arrived on the other side, they gave a sigh of relief.

The father stopped the wagon, climbed down, picked up some tools, and walked back to the bridge. He began to repair it. One of the children ran back to him crying, "Papa! Come on! We want to go!" But the father continued to work as he replied, "I must repair this old bridge so it will be ready for the next person who needs to cross."

The story, of course, is a parable of our lives. Often we are too much in a hurry, too preoccupied to deal with such things as rickety bridges. Let other people worry about them. Sometimes, however, our sense of responsibility tells us that the responsibility for action is ours—if only because nobody else has done anything about the problem. So we pause in our life's journey and respond to what needs to be done.

We have been reminded through our Bible study that Christ calls us not only to preach his gospel in words but to live it in our deeds. Like Jesus himself, we have a mission among the poor, the captives, the blind, the oppressed. As Christians, we are to be good Samaritans in our world. As the people of God, we are channels of God's justice and mercy. So far, so good. Let's assume that we are ready to respond. But is there really a need out there? What is there for us to do as we seek to translate our faith into action?

Many social problems cry out for solutions. Child abuse, for instance, is rampant; reported cases increased by 123 percent between 1976 and 1984. More and more families are going hungry, with approximately 14.5 percent below the poverty level—about half of them in households headed by women. The ranks of the homeless are increasing alarmingly. Welfare offices are inundated by persons seeking assistance. The crime rate is high. Drug use appears to be increasing. Teenage pregnancies abound. And these are only a few of the problems of our society. The multiplicity of challenges overwhelms us. Where shall we begin?

It may be helpful at this point to limit our consideration to a few groups that are frequently mentioned in the Bible as objects of God's special concern: the poor, the oppressed (especially women, children, and minorities), and the strangers within our land.

The Poor

"If there is among you a poor man, one of your brethren, in any of your towns within the land which the Lord your God gives you, you shall not harden your heart or shut your hand against your poor brother, but you shall open your hand to him, and lend him sufficient for his need, whatever it may be. . . ."

—Deuteronomy 15:7–8

Our personal values and experiences color the way we see the problems of the poor. Those of us who experienced the Great Depression in the 1930s, for instance, tend to have different benchmarks about poverty from those who have lived only in the more prosperous years since World War II. Likewise, as adults we continue to be influenced by the conditions under which we lived as children, whether in circumstances of affluence or of need.

In biblical times poverty was seen as the inevitable lot of certain classes of people, and this view continued for many centuries thereafter. The Reformation and the Industrial Revolution, however, have brought marked changes in our view of poverty and its stark reality over the past few hundred years. The Reformation gave birth to new ideas. Along with belief in salvation by grace, Christians began to interpret God's blessing to include material prosperity. If you were saved (some of them reasoned) you were blessed, and a sign of that blessing was financial gain. This led to the perverted idea that poverty meant you were not one of the elect, or else you were not following God as you ought. "Poverty and not idleness became the clear mark of moral depravity and moral failure."[21]

To examine the problems and needs of the poor requires us to set aside our own feelings and misconceptions. We must develop a strong sensitivity and compassion for human needs. We need to inform ourselves about conditions as they really are, to listen to the poor of today's world, to identify with them and to understand their situation. By building such bridges of understanding, we become more able to assist them in finding solutions to their poverty. Thus we are drawn closer to each other.

The Oppressed

"You shall not oppress your neighbor or rob him," the ancients were told in an Old Testament Book of Laws (Leviticus 19:13). This generalization is valid in all ages and all cultures, but in our modern society it seems particularly relevant to certain groups, such as women, children, and minorities.

Women

You shall not afflict any widow or orphan.

—Exodus 22:22

Biblical teachings about the welfare of widows are relevant today to a broader range of women than just those whose marriages have been broken by death. Our concern extends also to the divorced, the separated, and the unmarried, especially to those who are responsible for the care of children or who must cope with the problems of meager resources in their later years.

God commanded his people to care for widows and orphans, who were vulnerable in biblical times because they had no rights or privileges of their own. They lacked the protection of a husband or father. Today they are better protected by law (although there are still many inequalities). Nevertheless, the single mother and the elderly woman continue to be highly vulnerable in most societies. Customs, traditions, and even some laws of the land continue to work against many of them and condemn them to poverty.

Wider Opportunities for Women, Inc. (WOW) has reported that the social phenomena responsible for the feminization of poverty include:

—increased marital disruption in society
—inadequate benefits and support services for working mothers
—continuing barriers to employment opportunities for female workers
—low earnings of working women.[22]

What is our government doing about these conditions? We need to become familiar with programs that have assisted the single mother and her children in the past. Unfortunately in the United States, many of these programs have been severely cut back in funding, both at the federal and the state levels. Many programs aimed at providing employment, training, education, and equal access to jobs have been eliminated, even though they were effective in the past in helping women out of poverty and into self-sufficiency.

As for widows and older single women, they frequently find themselves trying to get by on meager funds. The income of most single women is well below that of single men in similar situations, and consequently their retirement benefits are also lower. To help the elderly widow or older single woman, we must first understand the uniqueness of their problems. As in Acts 6:1, we can become concerned about the needs and problems of women in unfortunate circumstances, and consider what actions of ours might help to improve their situation.

Children

> "God's curse on anyone who deprives foreigners, orphans, and widows of their rights." And all the people will answer, "Amen!"
>
> —Deuteronomy 27:19 (TEV)

The word "orphan" as it was once used needs to be redefined. In past times, an orphan was a child whose parents had died, and who therefore had nobody to take care of him or her except through some other family or an institution. Today we have fewer orphans by that definition, for parents live longer, and few boys and girls lose both of them during childhood because of death. Nevertheless, the basic problem of children cut off from their heritage and means of support remains, and in that sense we still have a great many orphans. Among the causes are these:

- Divorce
- Birth outside of marriage
- Mixed racial parentage
- Family crises which prevent children from remaining with parents
- Rejection of unmanageable children by their parents
- Child abuse
- Rebellion

All these factors, as well as others, lead to the presence of "unwanted" children in our society. We need to become aware of them in our communities. We share God's concern for them as we look for ways to assist them. We feel the need to make God's Good News real to them concerning Jesus, and to see that they have sufficient food and clothing, adequate housing, protection and nurture, and suitable adult companionship of both sexes.

Ethnic/Racial Minority Groups

> Oppressed people cannot remain oppressed forever. The urge for freedom will eventually come. This is what has happened to the American Negro. Something within has reminded him of his birthright of freedom; something without has reminded him that he can gain it.
>
> —Martin Luther King, Jr.[23]

The Civil Rights Act of 1964 brought an end to legal segregation, but blacks continue to be oppressed through more subtle forms of discrimination as well as open hostility. Black men and women consistently earn less than others in the labor force, and their efforts to secure integrated housing continue to meet with obstacles.

The history of blacks and whites in churches reveals the same story of discrimination. Blacks adopted Christianity as a result of Baptist and Methodist revivalism in the eighteenth and nineteenth centuries, and in the early years blacks and whites worshiped together in the same meeting houses, though often in separate parts of the room. Gradually, however, prejudice within churches forced a separation as the two groups moved into separate buildings, separate organizations, and finally into separate denominations. Out of their African religious roots and their experience as slaves, black churchmen developed an early form of what we would now call "liberation theology." The black church became a family of mutual support, the center of its community.

There is much that others can learn from the black church in general, and specifically from many dedicated black Christians. As blacks and whites we must listen to each other to bridge the gaps of racial prejudice that too often separate us. We can build on each other's strengths to form a closer community. We must respect our differences while we push aside our fears. Thus all of us will see each other as fellow humans created in the image of God.

Strangers Within Our Land

> Do not cheat a poor and needy hired servant, whether he is a fellow Israelite or a foreigner living in one of your towns.   —Deuteronomy 24:14 (TEV)

You shall not oppress a stranger . . . for you were strangers in the land of Egypt.

—Exodus 23:9

People who are "different" from ourselves in one way or another are particularly in need of our concern and care. There are many who qualify for this classification, but two of the principal groups are persons who have come from another country and people who are part of our tradition but do not fit easily into the culture of the majority.

Aliens and Immigrants

Important among those in our country who need our concern and care are the aliens and immigrants. Although these two groups are similar, they differ in that the immigrant has come to take up permanent residence and presumably apply for citizenship, whereas the alien maintains allegiance to the land of his or her birth. Through the years such persons have met with both hospitality and hostility in the United States—often simultaneously. Anglo-Saxons have had the easiest time because the colonies were settled mainly by persons from the British Isles, but other newcomers have often faced greater difficulties in proportion to the darkness of their skin color. Another factor has frequently been the degree of strangeness of their language, culture, and religious heritage.

The volume of immigration to the United States has varied over the years. During the years of rapid industrialization and expansion across the continent, people came in large numbers with the encouragement of the government. Periods of depression, however, led to restrictions of the flow of newcomers, as in 1882 when the Chinese Exclusion Act stopped the immigration of laborers willing to work for low wages.

Today the United States faces another immigration crisis, especially in the Southwest, which is the scene of many illegal crossings by aliens from Mexico and from Central and South America. As Christians we are faced with questions regarding these people. How should we respond to those who flee from economic hardship or political peril in countries to the south of us? How can we apply to this crisis God's commandments regarding aliens?

Strangers in Their Own Land

There are many who feel uncomfortable in the United States because they do not feel as though they "belong," even though it is the land of their birth. We have mentioned the black minority, and we might well add various other kinds of persons who are "different," perhaps because of physical or mental disabilities or some other unusual aspects of their personhood. Often overlooked, but certainly high on the list, are the American Indians, often referred to as Native Americans because they were here even before the white settlers.

Life has been hard for these people. Many tribes that had lived peacefully with the colonists were driven out of their ancestral lands and subjected to a cycle of removal, glowing promises, and broken treaties. In 1976 the Self-

Determination Act gave the tribes considerable control over services on the reservations. Major problems remain, however. Heavy reliance upon the federal government for money and resources subjects them to the whims of politicians. As funding decreases, tribal rights to water, land, and minerals become increasingly valuable, and these rights need to be protected.

Church involvement in Indian affairs has been both good and bad. Many past missionary efforts have increased the Indian's dependency upon whites. A Presbyterian study committee in 1985 observed that the government and the churches have worked hand–in–hand to Christianize and civilize the tribal people. Some would consider this process a mixed blessing at best. In the past we have established missions *to* the Indians, but now it is time to minister *with* them, to listen to them, to discover the problems they wish to address and the solutions they want to try.

The Importance of Bridges

Do you remember the sharecropper with whose story we began this chapter—the one who stopped in the midst of an important journey to go back and repair a rickety bridge? As Christians we are in the business of providing better bridges to persons who need our concern. Whether we build new bridges or repair old ones, we open the way to new opportunities and greater understandings. As we get to know one another across the chasms that have separated us from others, we discover how much alike we are. No matter what the group—needy women and children, others who live in poverty, persons of another race or national origin, strangers in our land, whoever they may be— we discover our ministry with each other as we seek God's forgiveness and message of hope.

Four congregations in Irvine, California, built a bridge of hope for each other: a Korean church, a Chinese church, an Assembly of God, and a traditional American Baptist church. Together they have developed a strong community ministry with shared facilities and a common witness. They function separately, yet occupy one building. They hold regular worship services separately but share special services and fellowship times. They learn from each other.

Participation in the Sanctuary Movement is also bringing churches together, both Catholic and Protestant, from a variety of socio-cultural, theological, and ethnic backgrounds. This is a movement to provide security through the churches for political refugees whose lives are endangered in their homelands. Christians are discovering that these bridges of hope have benefits not only for the refugees but also for those who offer them security and care. The fellowship of hope, in which people learn how to suffer with each other, becomes enriching. Sister Anna Marie, a sanctuary worker, has experienced these feelings. As she works with Central American refugees, listening to their testimony of life in violence–filled homelands, she joins them in standing before the Cross in the presence of a suffering Christ. There is resurrection, too, as they witness to the power of God's love and healing through those who are committed to help them.

Activities—
Uncovering Some Vital Issues

As we move on from our Bible study to some possible applications of our faith, we consider several specific issues that our biblical insights seem to address. Through continued group or individual study, we develop awareness and understanding of cultural perspectives and prepare to build relationships across cultural barriers. The activities include four suggested studies, each of which offers a number of options from which to choose.

Activity 1 studies issues related to the poor, helping us to experience the frustrations and powerlessness of poverty.

Activity 2 studies racial issues, offering insights through black history and a technique of listening.

Activity 3 studies issues involving aliens and immigrants and seeks ways to develop empathy with these people.

Activity 4 studies issues related to the Native American and suggests how people can work with each other.

Some Guidelines for These Activities

Important note: Some of these activities call for gathering information or sending away for materials that may be possible only if the leader looks ahead and plans several weeks in advance. "A word to the wise. . . . !"

If you are working in a group—

1. Continue to meet regularly for the next four studies.

2. Read the background material for each study.

3. Participate in discussions and exercises. Select the options that are most appropriate for your church's situation.

4. Accept the challenge of the assignments.

5. Encourage your pastor to read the information in these studies. Discuss ways of sharing your concerns for the poor, the oppressed, and the outcast in your community.

If you are studying individually—

Update your personal journal. Include your emotional responses to the exercises. Think of ways to share with other members of the church the new insights you are gaining.

Activity 1: Issues Facing the Poor

Background Information

Nearly 900,000 Americans fell below the poverty line in 1983, even though it was a period of economic recovery, according to a report of the Community Nutrition Institute.[25]

What does it mean to be poor? The federal government defines the level of poverty each year, based on changes in the consumer price index. This poverty index, originated by the Social Security Administration in 1964 (revised in 1969 and 1980) reflects the food consumption requirements of various families based on their size and composition. It is figured as a dollar amount, below which a family cannot meet its basic needs. Federal and state benefits such as food stamps, free school lunches, low-cost public housing, and Medicaid are paid according to this index. Many states, however, do not pay benefits at the current poverty level.

Federal assistance to needy children, originally called Aid to Dependent Children (ADC), began in 1935. At that time the maximum ADC payment was $18 per month per child. Coverage was extended in 1950 to include a needy parent or relative with whom the child lived. The food stamp program was started in 1960 to improve the diet of low-income households. A year later ADC became AFDC, or Aid to Families with Dependent Children, and assistance was permitted (if a state so elected) to families in which a father was in the home and unemployed.

The average length of time a family receives AFDC payments is approximately eighteen months. As a mother or father gets a job and the family moves above the poverty level, benefits are drastically cut or eliminated. Unfortunately, however, an emergency expense can abruptly reduce the family income below the poverty level again—a seesaw effect which makes it difficult to escape permanently from poverty.

Many poor adults and children fail to obtain the Recommended Daily Allowance (RDA) of basic nutrients. An inadequate diet hinders a child from developing physically, mentally, and emotionally. It often results in an increase of diseases and other medical problems. Hunger can therefore be called a national health epidemic among the poor.

The process for receiving federal and state welfare is cumbersome, time-consuming, and discouraging, and a common criticism is that welfare programs are crippled by cheating and fraud. If this is true, one must also bear in mind that cheating and fraud often appear on an even larger scale in other government programs such as military spending, farm subsidies, and education loans. As Christians we need to become informed regarding the level of poverty in our community (see Group Study: Option 1). We need to ask how eligibility is determined and how people can apply for benefits.

Group Study (choose one option)

Option 1

1. Experience individually or as a group what it is like to try to live on a poverty budget. Work it out on the form "Living on a Poverty Income" (Exhibit 1), dividing into subgroups of three or four persons if you have a large group. Check census figures or contact your local chamber of commerce to find out your community's income level. Contact your state welfare office to obtain the figure for AFDC payments and food stamp allotments for a mother with two children. Go through the budget twice: first, as if your income was one-half the average for your community; and, second, as you would have to do if you were reduced to living on an AFDC payment plus food stamps.

2. Against the background of your budgeting activity, discuss the following questions (or write your answers in your journal):

What kinds of supportive services would you need if you were trying to survive on a poverty budget?

How would you deal with unbudgeted emergencies?

How long could you live on a poverty budget before it would affect your mental health, making you anxious and depressed?

What would you do about medical costs if you moved above the legal poverty line and could no longer qualify for medical assistance?

What kinds of support would you like the church to provide, either through emergency relief or by working to change the system so it would provide for more effective assistance?

Option 2

If your group is already familiar with the problems of survival under a poverty budget, use this session to discuss your own sources of strength, such as family, neighborhood, church, and personal faith. List ways in which your church could help poor persons in the community to draw upon similar resources for help in survival on a poverty budget.

Option 3

Listen to the viewpoints of elderly people as they discuss their problems in trying to live on a limited budget. To do so, invite a panel of older persons from your church or community to describe their most pressing needs. Some questions to discuss with them:

Have any experienced a difference in earning power between men and women? Women & Employment, Inc., reported in 1981 that for every dollar earned by men, Hispanic women earned 49 cents, black women 54 cents, and white women 57 to 59 cents.[26]

EXHIBIT 1
Living on a Poverty Income

Instructions: In groups of three or four determine a monthly amount to spend in each category. This should be based upon your personal experience of what is an adequate but not excessive amount to spend in each category. Go through the exercise twice, once based on an average income and once for an AFDC income.* (For some items you may want to determine a yearly amount and divide by twelve to come up with a monthly figure.)

Item	Monthly Amount
Food	_____
Rent/House payment	_____
Utilities (gas, electric, water, phone)	_____
Medical costs (including medical insurance)	_____
Clothing	_____
Furniture/Appliances (cost and repair)	_____
Transportation, public or car, bicycle, etc. (includes cost, gasoline, maintenance, and insurance)	_____
Personal items (toiletries, cleaning supplies, paper goods, household goods)	_____
Laundry/Cleaning	_____
Entertainment (everyone needs some fun times—vacation, movies, dining out, baby-sitters)	_____
Day care or school costs	_____
Charitable and church contributions	_____
Miscellaneous expenses	_____
Total Monthly Budget	_____

*In Arizona, AFDC benefits in 1984 for a mother with two children were $233 per month. She could receive an additional $206 per month in food stamps and $8 low-income energy assistance for a total of $447 per month or $5,364 per year. The suggested poverty guideline for a family of three is $705 per month or $8,460 annually.

Source: Arizona Dept. of Economic Security, 1985.

EXHIBIT 2
A Litany of the Poor

Hearing the Word:
If there is among you a poor man, one of your brethren, in any of your towns within your land which the Lord your God gives you, you shall not harden your heart or shut your hand against your poor brother, but you shall open your hand to him, and lend him sufficient for his need, whatever it may be. [Deuteronomy 15:7-8]

Responding:
Hush, Lord! I know what I want. I've made plans and set a course. I haven't time or money.

Hearing the Word:
You shall not oppress a hired servant who is poor and needy, whether he is one of your brethren or one of the sojourners who are in your land within your towns. [Deuteronomy 24:14]

Responding:
Hush, Lord! It's dog eat dog out there. When did I get something except by work, and by sweat and cunning?

Hearing the Word:
When you give a dinner or a banquet . . . invite the poor, the maimed, the lame, the blind, and you will be blessed, because they cannot repay you. [Luke 14:12–13]

Responding:
Hush, Lord! I don't throw my things away. I have worked hard for what I have. They don't appreciate anything.

Hearing the Word:
I appeal to you therefore, brethren, by the mercies of God, to present your bodies as a living sacrifice, holy and acceptable to God, which is your spiritual worship. [Romans 12:1]

Responding:
Hush, Lord! Who am I to set the world right? Easy for you to say when it's my life and my plans at risk.

Hearing the Word:
He who sows sparingly will also reap sparingly, and he who sows bountifully will also reap bountifully. Each one must do as he has made up his mind, not reluctantly or under compulsion, for God loves a cheerful giver. [2 Corinthians 9:6, 7]

Responding:
Lord, call me louder! Is that your voice I hear, so still, so small? Is that your call in the pain of others that I am beginning to feel? Is it my destiny that is unfolding in the needs of those about me? Lord, call me louder!

The litany was written by the Rev. Lorimer Olson.

What community services do they consider to be the most helpful?

What groups in the community might be encouraged to serve as advocates for the elderly?

What can churches do to help them?

Group Project

Write a "Litany of the Poor," using selected Scriptures. (For an example, see Exhibit 2). Base your litany on your experience in the particular option you have chosen for study. If your pastor is willing, share the litany with the larger church family in some appropriate setting, so as to help others become sensitive to the social needs of people living in poverty. Encourage your pastor to preach on biblical social commandments and the social needs of your community.

Assignment

Ask everyone to read Luke 9:13–17 and meditate especially on Jesus' words in verse 13, "You give them something to eat." How would they relate their faith commitment to the act of responding to another person's hunger?

Activity 2: Problems of Blacks and Other Ethnic Minorities

Background Information

For more than two hundred years blacks and other ethnic minorities have tried to cope with racial and ethnic oppression in two ways. On the one hand they have attempted to become part of the dominant society through integration, and on the other hand they have chosen to remain separate. Integration is the process by which ethnic differences are submerged while cultural traits of the majority are imitated in an effort to become part of the society as a whole. Separatism seeks to resist majority-imposed social norms by restructuring minority groups and emphasizing differences with a renewed sense of pride. We will trace this wavering course as we look at black history in the United States.

It is believed that the first black people in America were brought into the Jamestown colony, probably by Dutch slave traders in 1619. Reliance on slave labor increased rapidly as the number and size of plantations grew in the South, and the black population increased. From early times the whites enforced a policy of social separateness, in which they often lived and worked in close proximity to each other, but never as equals. Restrictive laws and harsh punishments prevented violations of this code.

After the Emancipation Proclamation and the end of the Civil War, many blacks believed that integration would occur. The Thirteenth, Fourteenth, and Fifteenth amendments to the Constitution seemed to assure it. Integration failed, however, as the effect of those amendments was gradually nullified by later laws and rulings. Efforts were made to establish black colonies in unsettled areas of Florida and the West, and some blacks advocated a move back to Africa, but (except for Liberia and Sierra Leone) these efforts failed. Forced to accept their fate as a segregated minority, the majority of blacks became tenant farmers in the South or went north as low-paid laborers. They knew long periods of despair in which they were denied any feeling of self-worth by people who accepted the myths of black inferiority.

From suffering, minority groups often become stronger. Such was the case with blacks as, out of their suffering and despair, they began to develop a sense of cultural pride. This awareness was aided by the black church within the black community. The church provided the hub for mutual aid, welfare, and education. It counteracted the world with the message: "You are a person of worth and great value."

Segregation (separating or isolating blacks from the white society) was carried out through state and local laws, customs, and traditions, and often through fear of such hostile groups as the Ku Klux Klan. A policy of "separate but equal" developed, but it was seldom really equal. Nevertheless, this became a basic concept in the minds of most American citizens. Black people were thus allowed to remain "free" so long as they knew their place and stayed in it.

During the early 1900s many people, black and white, tried to be reconciled through integration. New organizations such as the National Association for the Advancement of Colored People began to work for integration of job opportunities, schools, and accommodations, as well as for voting rights.

In the late 1950s nonviolent civil disobedience developed in an effort to force integration. The Civil Rights Movement spread throughout the South and into many northern cities with sit-ins, school boycotts, picketing, freedom rides, voter registration, and marches. At the same time, separatism increased as many individuals began to favor revolutionary means to bring about equality. Today those who favored revolution appear to have run their course. In 1964 a Civil Rights Acts was passed, the first in eighty years on a national level, which gave blacks the full rights and privileges of citizenship, including voter registration, the use of public accommodations and public facilities, open schools and employment, and full access to federally assisted programs.

Whenever integration fails, the hurt and hostility of discrimination force minority groups to seek a safer world apart from white society. Separatism becomes important once more. Out of the conflicting struggles between integration and separatism has emerged a third way, known as racial and cultural pluralism. This approach seeks to combine the best from integration (equal opportunities) with the best of separatism (pride in one's cultural heritage). Many things have changed. Schools have become integrated, employment opportunities have opened, and the availability of housing has increased. Yet life remains very difficult for the majority of blacks and many other ethnic minorities. Oppression continues.

Getting Started

Ask the members to share their reactions to Jesus' words in Luke 9:13–17, as assigned in the previous session for study and meditation.

Group Study (choose one option)

Option 1: Group Discussion of Racism

1. Read the following quotation from Kenneth B. Clark and John Hope Franklin:

The chief barriers to racial justice today are subtle and much less conducive to media coverage. Such problems as inferior schools in northern cities that resist attempts at desegregation, deteriorating urban ghettos, persistent unemployment and underemployment, and the myriad handicaps of single-parent black families do not elicit the same moral indignation on the part of the American public as did earlier forms of injustice.[27]

2. Discuss the previous statement as it relates to your church and community. The discussion will vary according to whether yours is a black church, a white church, a small-town church, or an integrated church. List some subtle barriers to racial justice in your community. Discuss institutionalized racism (discrimination that has become so much a part of our lives that we are almost unaware of it). Think carefully of ways in which you might have "put down" others in the past without even realizing you were perpetuating racism, such as language, expectations, jobs, or jokes.

3. Set aside a time for prayer and confession to each other as you reaffirm your values in the worth of all God's creation and all its people.

Option 2: Practice in Communication

1. Discuss communication. What is it, and how is it accomplished? According to H. Stephen Glenn and Joel W. Warner, real communication includes a number of different skills: cooperating, negotiating, sharing, empathy, and listening.

2. Evaluate this quote from H. Stephen Glenn:

It is hard to communicate with people you don't understand, hard to negotiate with people whose position you can't imagine or understand, difficult to have empathy for people whose feelings you can't appreciate, difficult to cooperate with people you don't understand.

3. Practice interracial or interethnic communication by meeting one-to-one or in small clusters with people from a church of another racial or ethnic group who share common interests. For example: pastor with pastor, Sunday church school teacher with Sunday church school teacher, single mother with single mother, teenager with teenager, storekeeper with storekeeper, etc. Discover common problems and interests as well as those which may

be unique to one group or the other. As you begin to build an ecumenical feeling, try to add other churches to the dialogue.

Option 3: Learning How Others Have Fought Oppression

1. Contact other churches in your community or in other cities that have attempted to deal constructively with problems of prejudice and racism. Examples include:

Council of Churches of Greater Seattle, 4759 15th Avenue, N.E., Seattle, WA 89105. Churches in Seattle developed a model for urban ministry including an urban task force, ministry to the homeless, downtown housing, and city–wide conferences and workshops.

First Baptist Church, 111 West Monument, Dayton, OH 45402. This church developed a program to minister to the oppressed in their city and in El Salvador.

Allen Temple Baptist Church, 8500 A Street, Oakland, CA 94621. This church developed methods to bring power back into a declining community to fight oppression. For information see the book by G. Willis Bennett, *Effective Urban Church Ministry* (Nashville: Broadman Press).

(Your own local and state councils of churches or denominational offices may be able to offer additional suggestions.)

2. Study these materials and find ways to adapt their approaches in fighting oppression in your own community. Develop several ideas that you can share with your church family later. (Chapters 4 and 5 will suggest ways of sharing.)

Assignment

Ask each member to find a quiet place and read Psalms 23 and 103:6. Meditate on the goodness and righteousness of God. Reflect on God's activity in the lives of his people. Consider God's special concern for the oppressed.

Activity 3: Immigrants and Aliens in the Community

Background Information

Immigration has dramatically increased in the United States since 1975. In fact, as an article in *Time* has stated, "an amazing two-thirds of all the immigration in the world consists of people entering the U.S."[29] Many people do not receive them with very great enthusiasm, however. The same article, commenting on the differences in origins, religions, and lifestyles of these newcomers, explains that most Americans do not know what to make of them:

> 59% believe that immigrants generally end up on welfare (the best estimate is that less than 20% do), and 54% think they add to the crime problem. Yet 58% feel that immigrants are basically good, honest people, and 67% think they are productive citizens once they become established.[30]

This quotation emphasizes our conflicting ideas and impressions of immigrants and aliens. In order to understand these newcomers coming into our communities, we need to know more about them.

Immigration today is very different from that of an earlier generation. No longer do immigrants come by ship to Ellis Island but they arrive by airplane, automobile, small boat, and "over the fence" to widely scattered locations. Immigrants have concentrated their settlement mainly in urban and suburban areas of six states: California, New York, Texas, Florida, Illinois, and New Jersey. Every part of the United States, however, has been affected. Sponsorship by churches and other organizations and individuals has brought these people into communities all over the nation, and some of them have later moved to other locations which they preferred because of climate, work opportunities, or friends.

Today's flood of immigration comes from all parts of the world, with the majority coming from underdeveloped countries. Each year about one-half million immigrants enter the United States legally, and many more illegally. The *Time* article already cited says that there are four major categories of immigrants living in New York City: European and Middle Eastern, Hispanic, Caribbean, and Asian and Pacific.

Immigrants or aliens have fears of the unknown when they enter a new land. Often they have been forced to leave most of their possessions in the old country. Many times they have left a loved one behind. In their new homeland they become faced with the problem of survival. "Can we find a place to live? Can we learn a new language? Can we find a job?"

Established Americans are also fearful. They are not sure about these new and different people. They too are nervous about their own survival. "Will this country be overrun by aliens? Will my way of life be changed? Will I be harmed in some way?"

In addition to legal immigration, many come illegally, but nobody knows how many. Their number can only be guessed at.

> The Census Bureau . . . estimated the total of illegal immigrants in the U.S. at between 3.5 million and 6 million in 1978 . . . Roughly 60% of the illegals are Hispanics, and about two-thirds of these are Mexicans driven by poverty and unemployment across the highly porous 2,000-mile southern frontier.[31]

There are opposing opinions regarding illegal immigration and how it affects the American economy. Many people believe that illegal, undocumented workers create more money by increasing production, tax money, and commerce. Others think they take more money from the community, through their use of community services and welfare aid, than they give. Charles P. Alexander comments in *Time:* "About the only thing the experts agree on is that illegal immigration is a boon for employers and consumers." And Sidney Weintraub, professor of international affairs at the University of Texas, concludes: "Some people are hurt by illegal aliens and some benefit."[32]

Churches and church members are becoming embroiled in this controversy. Some believe that we must limit immigration and severely penalize not only those who enter illegally but those who help them. Others feel that Christians have a duty to speak out against injustice and suffering in the lives of troubled aliens. Wherever we are as individuals in our thinking on this issue, we need to remain open to the needs of persons outside our country who seek freedom and hope.

Before we can relate to any aliens or immigrants, we must understand them. We can do this only as we learn to listen to their cry. Says John Bachman: "Christian love . . . is not simply a task a person decides to undertake . . . . It is God's love—revealed in his marvelous acts, assurances, and promises—that is reflected in our own acts of love."[33]

I asked my friend Josefina to tell me how she became involved in helping illegal aliens or undocumented workers from Mexico and El Salvador. She said she did not set out to become so involved, but God has called her, she believes, to respond to persons in need. Her story begins with a small incident involving a child:

> One Thanksgiving Day my church, a small inner-city Hispanic congregation, decided to share a big holiday dinner with some Central American immigrants. I was serving the food. Among those coming along the food line was a very small Salvadoran girl about six years of age. She took an adult portion of everything until her plate was completely full. Soon she was back for another full plate. I was concerned that she might get sick, but I let her fill her plate. Before long, the little girl was back for the third time, waiting to be served everything again. This time I was afraid to give her any more.
>
> I explained to the child that she would get sick if she ate any more, but she did not say a word. She just stood there waiting. Finally I understood that she was speaking to me in her own way, but that I had failed to hear her. Through her silence she was saying, "I know what it is like to be hungry." I realized that I had never been truly hungry. It was from my plenty that I was judging, not from her hunger.

How often do we react to someone out of our own experience because we have failed to understand theirs? Only a bridge of hope can bring us together.

Getting Started

Recall the readings from the Psalms assigned in the previous session. Share with the group (or write in your own journal) your praises for God's goodness. Continue in a special prayer time to bring the needs of the oppressed before the Lord.

Group Study (choose one option)

Option 1: Personal Experiences with Immigrants

1. Recall some actual experiences you have had with immigrants or aliens in the past few years. Ask others to do the same. Would you describe these experiences as positive or negative? Why? What is your gut reaction to the increased immigrant population? What do you believe immigrants have contributed to our communities?

2. Share (or record in your journal) any personal experiences your ancestors may have had as immigrants. Discuss lessons which they learned that can help you empathize with today's immigrants.

3. Think about Leviticus 19:33: "When a stranger sojourns with you in your land, you shall not do him wrong." How does God want us to react to immigrants and aliens?

4. Discuss what your church could do to help your community take a more positive step toward accepting immigrants and aliens.

Option 2: The Central American Problem

1. Discuss (or think about) the following statement:

> First, we should seek to understand the content of our neighbor's cry. In this society we are conditioned by the media to hear and see suffering without probing deeply into its content . . . Second, we should respond by acknowledging our share of responsibility. We need to recognize that our neighbors' hardship has been created, in part, by the U.S.

2. Read Exhibit 3, "Keeping the Backyard Safe." Of the military actions the United States has taken in Central America and the Caribbean, which of them were conducted primarily to protect Uncle Sam's interest?

3. Discuss the fact that American businesses and banks have invested heavily in Central America and the Caribbean. What in your opinion is their incentive? Obviously they have received a good dollar return, or they would not have made these investments. What do you think would happen in those countries if profits were to decline or vanish? To make this possibility more real, see whether you can find someone in your community who was employed by a business that shut down its operations, and discuss with that person what the experience was like.

4. Discuss: What can we do as Christians to address the problems of immigrants and aliens in our land? How could our church make them feel more welcome? Do we need to confess our sins as members of a sinful society?

5. If the church might be interested in the Sanctuary Movement, send for material on it. Suggested references include:

The Chicago Religious Task Force on Central America, 1020 South Wabash Avenue, Room 401, Chicago, IL 60605–2215.

"Crucible of Hope" Sojourners, P.O. Box 29272, Washington, DC 20017.

Option 3: Impact of Immigrants and Aliens on Our Own Community

1. Review the U.S. Census figures for any changes in ethnic population in your state.

2. Check with city officials to discover what changes, if any, they have noted.

3. Discuss: Where do recent immigrants and aliens in this community come from, and where are they living?

4. Investigate whether there are any organizations in this community working with these new groups. Talk to persons who run the organizations. Learn how they view the problems. (Possible sources of information: United Way or council of social agencies.)

5. Discover the needs and what a church can do to help meet them.

6. Acknowledge your own fears and overcome them through prayer.

Assignment

Before the next session meditate on James 2:15–17. Ask in prayer what God wants you to do to help someone.

Activity 4: Learning How to Work with Each Other

Background Information

When we begin to move outside our church fam-

EXHIBIT 3
Keeping the Backyard Safe

"In the commitment of freedom and independence, the peoples of this hemisphere are one. In this profound sense we are all Americans. Our principles are rooted in self-government and non-intervention."

President Ronald Reagan,
February 24, 1982

"I spent 33 years and four months in active service as a member of the . . . Marine Corps . . . . And during that period I spent most of my time being a high-class muscle man for Big Business . . . . Thus I helped make Mexico and especially Tampico safe for American oil interests in 1914. I helped make Haiti and Cuba [decent places] for the National City Bank to collect revenues in . . . I helped purify Nicaragua for the international banking house of Brown Brothers in 1909 to 1912. I brought light to the Dominican Republic for American sugar interests in 1916. I helped make Honduras 'right' for American fruit companies in 1903."

Major General Smedley D. Butler,
writing in 1935

The following is a list of U.S. military interventions in Central America and the Caribbean from 1898 to the present. Most were undertaken to protect U.S. property and business interests during times of political upheaval or instability. The list does not include the several U.S. incursions into Mexico during the same period.

1898–1902 Cuba. Military occupation following the Spanish-American War.

1898 Nicaragua. To protect American lives and property at San Juan del Sur.

1899 Nicaragua. To protect U.S. interests during an insurrection.

1901 Colombia (State of Panama). To protect U.S. property during revolutionary disturbances.

1902 Colombia (State of Panama). To keep railroad lines open across the isthmus.

1903 Honduras. To protect the U.S. consulate and shipping facilities during revolutionary activity.

1903 Dominican Republic. To protect U.S. interests in Santo Domingo during a revolutionary outbreak.

1903–1914 Panama. To protect U.S. interests during U.S.-engineered revolution for independence from Colombia and the building of the Canal.

1904 Dominican Republic. To protect U.S. interests during revolutionary fighting.

1905 Honduras. Marines landed at Puerto Cortez.

1906–1909 Cuba. To restore order after revolutionary activity.

1907 Honduras. To protect U.S. interests during a war between Honduras and Nicaragua.

1910 Nicaragua. On three occasions during a civil war.

1911 Honduras. To protect U.S. interests during a civil war.

1912 Honduras. To prevent government seizure of a U.S.-owned railroad.

1912 Panama. To supervise elections outside the Canal Zone.

1912 Cuba. To protect U.S. interests in the province of Oriente and Havana.

1912–1925 Nicaragua. To protect U.S. interests during an attempted revolution and to maintain stability afterwards.

1914 Haiti. To protect U.S. citizens during unrest.

1914 Dominican Republic. Gunships deployed during a revolutionary movement.

1915–1934 Haiti. To maintain order during a period of chronic insurrection.

1916–1924 Dominican Republic. To maintain order during a period of chronic insurrection.

1917–1923 Cuba. To protect U.S. interests during an insurrection and to maintain order afterwards.

1919 Honduras. To maintain order during an attempted revolution.

1920 Guatemala. To protect U.S. interests during fighting between unionists and the government of Guatemala.

1921 Panama-Costa Rica. U.S. naval squadron stationed on both sides of the isthmus to prevent a boundary war.

1924 Honduras. To protect U.S. interests during election hostilities.

1925 Honduras. To protect foreigners during political upheaval.

1926–1933 Nicaragua. To suppress revolutionary activities led by Augusto Sandino after a military coup. Occupation ended with the installation of Anastasio Somozo as president.

1932 El Salvador. U.S. warships stand by offshore during a peasant rebellion and subsequent massacre of 30,000 peasants.

1933 Cuba. Naval forces deployed during a revolution. No landing was made.

1954 Guatemala. Military coup planned, organized, and financed by U.S. Central Intelligence Agency.

1961 Cuba. Bay of Pigs invasion planned, organized, and financed by CIA.

1965 Dominican Republic. 20,000 troops directed by the CIA.

1981–? Nicaragua. Covert war funded and directed by the CIA.

1983 Grenada. Invasion by 6,000 U.S. troops to establish a new government during a time of political instability.

The above list was primarily compiled from *Empire as a Way of Life*, by William Appleman Williams. Oxford University Press, 1980; *Under the Eagle*, by Jenny Pearce, Latin American Bureau, 1981; and *A People's History of the United States*, by Howard Zinn, Harper & Row, 1980. Revised from the April 1982 issue of *Sojourners*.

ily environment, we meet people who appear to be different, and we may find ourselves trying to change them to be just like ourselves. The historical approach to our dealings with the Native American illustrates this fact.

Indians migrated to the American continent perhaps as early as 25,000 B.C. By the time Columbus arrived, hundreds of tribes had developed their unique and complex cultures throughout North America. As English, French, and Spanish began to settle, they established relationships with the Indians. Cooperation with friendly tribes was necessary at first, because their help was crucial for protection against other Indians who were more hostile, and because they could be drawn into alliances for warfare among the three European powers. Later, as land was taken over by the settlers, Indians were less "needed" and were forced to yield to the expanding frontier. From the beginning the white man's policy toward the Indian seems to have been: "You must assimilate into the white culture or die." Many laws regarding the Indians were based on "protecting" them because they would not assimilate. By the early 1800s, Americans became convinced that it was their "manifest destiny" to settle the frontier, moving it constantly westward and forcing the Indian to relocate beyond it.

As their ancestral lands were taken away, Indians lost their means of livelihood and became increasingly dependent upon the government for the necessities of life. Reservations were established as their new homelands. The U.S. Bureau of Indian Affairs, formed in 1824, became the guardian of these people, establishing a policy of dependency in which the government was the parent and the Indian was the child.

When the settlers met the American Indians, two worlds collided. The settlers came from a basically Christian tradition that stressed individual freedom. The Christians knew God as Father, Son, and Holy Spirit, who had created humans and had a personal relationship with them. They believed that man and woman had fallen into 'sin and thus had brought a curse on all creation, and they believed further in a final judgment after death. The Indians, on the other hand, believed differently. Their tradi-

tion placed the community above the individual. Some Indians believed they came from the earth. They believed in God, but as part of the community rather than personal. Mother Earth was more real to them than a Heavenly Father. They believed that everything was good and that human beings must be in balance with nature. Their worship was closely tied in with other aspects of tribal customs.

Missionary efforts with Indians have followed various approaches. In the Southwest, for instance, Pueblo civilization was compatible with that of the Spanish Catholics in that both stressed ceremonies, rituals, and priestly leadership. The Pueblos, therefore, adapted to Spanish civilization somewhat by adding Catholic symbols to their native religion. On the other hand, the Indian culture of New England was very different from that of the Puritans. The Indians there found it hard to accept the preaching of human depravity which Puritan missionaries offered. More successful, at least in the beginning, were the efforts of the Moravians in the middle Atlantic area, who encouraged Indians to build on their community values by developing communal villages near the Moravian settlements, each complete with a school and a church. These Indian villages, however, were destroyed later when whites refused to accept them as part of the larger community.

As we look at these beginnings, we see that mission to Indians was to a people who were considered "different" and who, according to European standards, needed to become "civilized." Settlers viewed the Indians as lazy and lacking in ambition because they resisted pressure to adopt their philosophy and lifestyle. Therefore in 1818 President Madison approved a plan to provide federal support for church missions, hoping that thus the Indians would become both civilized and Christianized through a common effort. Most white people expected that the Indians would then begin to act like them, but no such thing happened. Life for Indians became more restrictive and difficult, and many of the missionaries tried to alleviate their suffering and hardship.

The government allocated various Indian reservations to specific Christian denominations who were given ground on which to construct missions, schools, and medical facilities. Commendable as these efforts were, however, they often backfired by teaching the Indians to become more dependent. The missions tended to be paternalistic, thus weakening the traditional leadership roles of the chiefs.

Schools became an important part of mission work. In many cases these were boarding schools, established off the reservations to teach vocational skills. Often, however, operating funds were too meager to accomplish their goals as fully as intended (or sometimes even to provide an adequate diet). In the 1890s the federal government entered the boarding school field, but little thought seems to have been given to helping Indians develop leadership skills, and thus their dependency increased. The good of the boarding schools seems to have been offset by their harmful effect on Indian family life. A Presbyterian study reports that the separation of large numbers of children from their homes "began to fracture the Indian homes and took away the responsibility of parenthood."[35]

Approximately one-fourth of all American Indians now live on reservations. Most reservations are small, usually having not more than a thousand persons. Few states east of the Mississippi River have Indian populations of more than ten thousand. Just four states—California, Arizona, New Mexico, and Oklahoma—together have 46 percent of the total Indian population. There are Indian reservations and villages, however, even in the East.

Indians have managed to survive despite many efforts to force them to assimilate. Most of them continue to resist full assimilation, preferring "acculturation" as a response to a non-Indian society. Thus they adapt to white culture but hang onto parts of their own heritage. Caught between the competing pulls of the reservation and of the city, some 700,000 of them have broken away and live in urban areas, yet many of them long to return to reservation life when they get enough money together. A large number move back and forth between city and reservation as they become disillusioned in turn with each.

The modern response by whites to Indians continues to focus on our differences. As a result, Indians continue to be little known or understood. Says Vine Deloria, Jr.: "Indians remain an exotic and unknown quantity. The quality and pathos of their lives remain unexamined and beyond the concern of most Americans."

Getting Started

Recall the assignment to think about James 2:15–17. What spiritual experiences or new ideas did this provide?

Group or Individual Study

We examine Indians and other groups who may need our understanding, in an effort to find ways for us to begin working together with them. Choose one of the following options as you prepare to establish a relationship with a group in your community.

Option 1: Your Church's Mission with American Indians

1. Discuss (or consider) how your church participates in mission work with Native Americans. Find out whether the work is limited to either reservation or nonreservation Indians.

2. Find out what type of approach this missionary effort takes. In the past most mission work was *to* or *for* the Indian. Today it is beginning to shift to working *with* the Indian. Test against this statement by Dr. R. Pierce Beaver:

> Modern mission thought is based on three points: (1) faith should reflect people's culture, (2) missionaries should be aware of local cultural and religious values, and (3) missionaries and local leaders should work together guiding change in local culture.

(Write to your missionaries or your denominational offices to receive information concerning their policies and programs. Numerous pamphlets are available through the Board of National Ministries, American Baptist Churches, U.S.A., Valley Forge, PA 19482-0851.)

3. Find out how your mission dollar is spent. How many native or indigenous church leaders are involved in the mission program? How are they trained? What could your church do to help provide scholarship money to support the training of native leaders?

Option 2: Local or State Policies Toward American Indians

1. If you live in an area with an Indian population, what do you know about their problems or goals? Discover the extent of the Indian population by looking at census records and/or talking with state or local officials.

2. If you live in an area with a large Indian population, investigate some of the problems that remain to be solved for Indians living on reservations. These may include unemployment, inadequate medical care on the reservation, overcrowded housing, and the need for quality education for children on the reservation (to keep the family together). Plan a visit to the nearest reservation, if possible. Meet tribal leaders and missionaries. Hear what they say about the needs. Discuss whether Indian leaders are seeking to become self-sufficient. Find out what you can about politics in your locality regarding Indian lands, treaties, and problems (get more than one point of view).

3. Bring the information back to the group and lead a discussion on how your church can promote an Indian viewpoint.

4. Search for Indian missions in your community. Ask your denomination for information on urban ministries with Indians. Check your local telephone directory for Indian missions. Talk to leaders involved in urban mission efforts and discover their needs. See how you can support them.

5. Tell your group about Kip and Ollie Heth, a dedicated young married couple, both ordained ministers, who have been working in an urban Indian ministry established by an American Indian minister who has since moved on to become pastor of an Indian church in Montana. Kip and Ollie urge churches to promote an awareness of the Christian Indian community within the larger urban Indian community. Although community resources are often needed, say the Heths, Christians should not just look for things they can *give* the urban Indians, but should build bridges of understanding and cooperation.

They suggest that non-Indian residents look for ways to assist urban Indians to move from menial jobs to work that requires more skill and profession-alism. A church could provide valuable help by establishing a day care center for Indian children whose parents must work. Creative ministry with urban Indians will seek to develop new ways of promoting Christian love and fellowship. Non-Indian Christians must be willing to accept servant roles toward Indians when appropriate. For example, instead of teaching Bible to Indians, non-Indian Christians might offer to care for Indian babies and young children while Indian parents meet with an Indian teacher for Bible study.

Option 3: A Variety of Community Problems

1. You may live in a community where residents are failing to understand problems of certain other special groups of people. Here are a few examples. You may discover others.

In the 1980s the American farmer is facing new economic and social problems. Take time to listen.

Ethnic groups continue to encounter misunderstanding and hostility as they seek to move into some communities. What do you know personally about such problems in your community?

Group homes for children or adults with disabilities and social problems often become targets for attack. Are there any of these where you live? Examine the issues. Discover the fears that surround the problem. Listen to the pros and cons of people involved.

2. Determine for yourself how to respond to problems like these. Become sensitive. Promote harmony. Take a stand for justice. Encourage your church to sponsor open discussions with persons who have opposing points of view.

3. Study the Scriptures to seek God's guidance. Many of the passages already mentioned in the activities of Chapters 1 and 2 are appropriate for review at this point.

Assignment

The final meditation for this group of studies is Matthew 25:34–40. Each member should read it and think about it.

What do these words mean to you personally? *To be a follower we must put our love into action. Love toward another equals love toward God.*

3

Developing an Awareness of Needs

Lord God, in every nation you are calling out people and training them by faith to be a blessing to all the families of the earth. Help us to be true to our identity and unite our efforts to hasten that day when your plan is completely fulfilled.

—Linnea Okasaki Foss[38]

God is calling us to a ministry of love that leads into action. We have studied God's commandments and looked at how Jesus modeled a lifestyle of active love and concern for others. We have seen the history of oppression in this country as it has affected various groups of people, and we have viewed oppression and poverty as they exist in many communities today. Now we want to discover the tasks God has waiting for us.

First of all, let us look at a commandment found in both the Old and New Testaments, "You shall love your neighbor as yourself" (Leviticus 19:18 and Luke 10:27). To understand how we are to love our neighbor, we need to reflect on how God has loved us. This insight will enable us to love ourselves with a wholeness and a balance that permit us truly to love others.

To minister effectively to persons in need we begin by identifying our own sins and needs. We then reaffirm the source of our salvation and our ministry. Before we become involved in redemptive activity, however, we need to turn our hearts and minds inward to examine our own sins and motives. In so doing, we may hear the voice of God directing us toward certain areas of concern. Persons committed to ministry through community action should prepare by spending some time regularly for a few weeks in prayer, meditation, and quiet listening to the voice of God. They are most likely to stick to the discipline if they spend a specific time period each day listening to God, and then meet with others weekly to reaffirm their faith and rejoice in the knowledge of salvation.

Since a church is a whole made up of many parts, each of us must ask, "What is *my* personal role as a member of God's fellowship in society, and how do I fulfill that role?" Our answer will grow out of our faith—our faith in God's gift of salvation for the human race through the sacrificial death of Jesus on the cross. As each of us accepts that gift individually, this faith guides us to witness, love, and minister in Jesus' name according to our own unique gifts. By searching ourselves we sense the calling that leads us from faith to action. Our faith propels us to minister to others in love and understanding.

Perhaps up to this point in our lives we have followed God without experiencing the call to action. Now, however, things are different. We become so aware of the world and its needs that we no longer can go about our daily routine in the same manner as before. Faith, we realize, cannot be separated from action. In the words of John Bachman, "A faith involving no work on my part allows me to think only of God serving me instead of my being a servant of God." With an action-related faith we can begin to consider ways of helping individuals whom previously we may have overlooked.

Sometimes churches become ivory towers, sheltering their members from the world. Their approach to social problems has been to try to decrease their visibility. Out of sight for them becomes out of mind. If we are to see, hear, and feel the world around us differently, we must look and listen carefully and deliberately. To do this, we must push our fears aside. First, however, we need to identify these fears and then work through them so that they no longer block our way. Here are some of the fears that may confront us as we begin to move out of our safe environments, our private ivory towers:

The fear of failure. Most of us are afraid of failing. Therefore we tend to stay where we have already succeeded, where we feel secure. To push this fear aside, we need to regard the new not as a threat but as a challenge.

The fear of persons different from ourselves. We may be afraid of people who are unlike us in their social class, racial background, way of thinking, or other characteristics. Another word for this fear is "prejudice." We can work to reduce it by broadening and deepening our contacts with others so that we come to know them as they really are.

The fear of new experiences. We like the calm waters of routine. We are reluctant to move into uncharted new experiences. Our response to this must be to learn to be adaptable. As we test the more turbulent waters to which we are challenged, we find that we are better able to deal with them than we expected.

The fear of feeling like an outsider. Like self-conscious adolescents we cling to our old friends rather than risk the possible embarrassment of being outsiders in new groups. To work on this fear, we need to take our minds off ourselves and begin to concentrate on others and their needs.

The fear of danger. The path ahead has its pitfalls, so we avoid it by telling ourselves, "God surely does not want me to go there!" We can challenge this fear by recognizing that just the opposite is often true. It is God's strength and guidance that enable us to go ahead.

When we fail to face our fears, we usually turn them into anger, or we become defensive or too busy to do what we ought to do. Whatever our fears, we can proceed only as we face them and thrust them aside. Our prayer must be:

"The Lord is my helper,
I will not be afraid;
what can man do to me?"

—Hebrews 13:6

You may already have begun to discover your community as you participated in the cultural studies suggested by the Activities section of Chapter 2. Now you need to decide what to do about your discoveries, but this may not be easy. You may feel very much like a certain young minister who had just accepted a call to a new pastorate in a changing neighborhood. He made it his priority goal to talk with people in the area—people who were not related to his church—people who were "different." He tried to understand their problems. Within him grew a burning desire to reach out to them with the Good News by first becoming a good neighbor. He wanted these people to know that the church cared about them as individuals; he wanted to become partners with them to work on community problems. He urged church members to join him in visiting these neighborhood families in order to cultivate a strong bond of friendship between the two groups. However, the church people were afraid at first. They could not accept this goal until they, too, had begun to "experience" the neighborhood in a new way as their pastor had.

You may be a pastor or layperson wanting to move out into your community to do God's work. The first step is to set aside your preconceived ideas of the people who live there—to look at them with new eyes and listen to them with new ears. We must become sensitive to their problems and needs as we seek to "bear one another's burdens" (Galatians 6:2).

A group of suburban laypeople belonging to a downtown church moved the church to a newer growth area and began to meet weekly to learn how to discern the old neighborhood with new understanding. Dividing the area around the church into four parts, they set out to become reacquainted with the places where they had once lived. They were surprised as they learned about the needs and the pains people experienced in each of these locations. As the group became more sensitive, it expanded its horizon of interest and concern. As the contrasting needs of the old and new communities became real to them, their hearts turned again to the downtown neighborhood they had known and loved in years past.

The Activities section suggests three books to help you in your prayer and meditation experiences. Wherever you are in your growing knowledge of the church neighborhood, these activities are designed to help you increase your understanding.

Activities—
Community Awareness

To become better acquainted with the challenges and opportunities which our community offers for Christian ministry, we take a look first at ourselves and then at the neighborhood around our church, and finally we put it all together.

Activity 1 leads us to an inward journey of prayer and meditation.

Activity 2 enables us to study our community in depth.

Activity 3 brings together what we have done as we compile and analyze our findings.

Some Guidelines for These Activities
If you are working in a group—

1. Set aside a specific time period for group members to participate in an inner journey of prayer and meditation. Ask: "What is God calling us to do in this community?"

2. Following the prayer time, form your group into a task force committed to action in the area to which you feel called. Plan to meet on a regular basis for one or more months.

3. Select a leader for the group and someone to take notes regarding decisions, assignments, and reports.

4. Seek your pastor's counsel. Keep the pastor informed.

5. Begin to build a relationship between the task force and your church's governing board or other leaders. As a first step, develop a short statement regarding your group's activities and its interest in the community. Present it to the appropriate body and ask to have your group officially recognized by the church.

If you are working as an individual—

1. Set aside a specific time for an inward journey of prayer as you seek God's call to action.

2. Select some constructive activities that you can do by yourself and consider how you might develop them into a community witness project.

3. Discuss your proposed project with your pastor. How might you activate it, either working alone or with the help of others? Firm up your plans.

4. Undertake the project in the faith that God is preparing others to work with you.

Activity 1: Taking an Inner Journey of Prayer and Meditation

Select a book relating faith to action, which each person can read and study during prayer time. Here are three suggestions:

Confession and Forgiveness, by Andrew Murray (Grand Rapids: Zondervan Publishing House, 1978). This book of thirty-three meditations on Psalm 51 is suitable for a month–long study. Originally published in 1896, it may be difficult for some to read because of its old–fashioned approach to human guilt and degradation, but many will find it worth the effort.

Speech, Silence, Action, by Virginia Ramey Mollenkott (Nashville: Abingdon Press, 1980). Mrs. Mollenkott takes the reader through three steps in the cycle of faith that are necessary for action to occur.

Activity 2: Taking a Careful Look at the Community

Begin by making a survey of the neighborhood in its various aspects.

1. Define the boundaries of two areas: the specific local neighborhood within the influence of your church building and the broader community in which the congregation lives. Show these on a map, using a distinctive shading or color to indicate the

former and colored map pins to identify the latter. "A church is both a building and a congregation of members. Many congregations fail to make an impact on their community because they have never defined that area."[40]

2. Divide your neighborhood among the task force members, and have them walk or drive around it singly or in pairs to get a really close up look at it. They should record their observations on copies of Exhibit 4, "Windshield Survey Information Sheet."[41] Remember that the goal is to discover persons who need love and concern.

3. Get in touch with your senses, such as sight, hearing, smell, and even the "sixth sense" of intuition. Discuss or write down your answers to these questions:

• From looking: How do the people I pass on the street or in the stores look? Happy? Discouraged? Harried? How are they dressed? What kinds of people do I see? Children? Elderly people? Mostly men or mostly women? What races or ethnic groups do they represent? What are they doing?

• From listening: Do I hear anyone laughing, crying, shouting? Is there oppressive noise pollution, or quiet and peace? What do these sounds tell me?

• From sniffing: What kinds of odors do I notice? Smog? Flowers? Industrial smells? Pine trees? Rotting garbage? Stale beer? What do these suggest?

• From intuition: Does the neighborhood seem warm and friendly or cold and forbidding? Is it a pleasant place in which to be?

4. This involves going in pairs or individually to do personal interviewing in the community. The interviews may occur spontaneously as you meet people, or they can be structured to include appointments with specific community leaders and resource people. It will be helpful to use Exhibit 5, "Community Questions," though perhaps not too conspicuously. As you ask your questions, listen both to the facts and to the feelings expressed. Be alert to nonverbal communication such as eye contact (or lack of it), tone of voice, friendly or cool responses. Record your impressions.

5. Obtain statistical information from census reports at the library or from other sources such as the chamber of commerce and the county or city planning and zoning offices. You may find it helpful to use Exhibit 6, "Statistical Information," to record your findings and Exhibit 7, "Analyzing the Statistical Data,"[42] to draw conclusions from them.

6. Discover the history of your community and record it on a copy of Exhibit 8, "History of the Community."[43] Sources include the library and the chamber of commerce or tourist bureau. Many communities have developed promotional material, including perhaps historical brochures for some special celebration. Another source of history is personal interviews with longtime residents, especially governmental officials or leaders of community organizations (perhaps now retired).

Activity 3: Compiling and Analyzing the Findings

Using Exhibits 5–8, plus any informal reports of impressions brought in by interviewers, compile and analyze the findings of the group. Prepare to put them to use as tools for community ministry.

1. Determine how the material you have put together can help your church as it moves into community ministry.

2. Develop a written report that can be distributed to the entire church membership. This could be tied in with a visual presentation, using the community map on which you have shown with shading or color the church's "ministry neighborhood" and with map pins the church membership. Include in the report the results of your research in Activity 2, with your own impressions of it. It should be reinforced with interesting and specific information from the questionnaire, statistics, and community history, and should conclude with significant findings and recommendations.

3. Rejoice together in the work of the task force. Recount your experiences as a group (or record them in your personal journal). Include statements about how your feelings about the neighborhood or community may have changed. Share your awareness of God's presence and power as you have tried to become acquainted with the community.

EXHIBIT 4
Windshield Survey Information Sheet

AREA COVERED _____

GENERAL LAYOUT
   Street and traffic patterns _____

_____

   Physical boundaries _____

_____

   Identifying marks _____

_____

   Characteristics of the area _____

_____

_____

HOUSING PATTERNS
   Kinds of housing _____

_____

   Clustering of housing _____

_____

   General appearance _____

_____

_____

INTERRELATIONS
   Signs of people relating _____

_____

   General impressions of population (age, activity) _____

_____

_____

EXHIBIT 5
Community Questions*

What boundaries are there in the community?

How many people live there?

What is the population breakdown by: Ethnicity
Income
Age
Occupations
Households

What kinds of resident businesses?/How many?

What form of government?

What kinds of service organizations?/How many?

Where do people work?

Where do people play?/What recreation facilities are available?

What kinds of churches?/How many?

What kinds of bars?/How many?

What kinds of volunteer associations?/How many?

What kinds of neighborhoods?/How many?

What kind of police department is there?

What are the boundaries of school district(s)?

Are schools coincident with community boundaries?

Is there a PTA? Is it active?

What is the local political situation?

Do issues cut across large or small populations?

Is there a community land-use plan?

What social welfare services are available?

Hospital/Medical?   Social services?
Private for profit?   State services?
Private nonprofit?   Federal services?

What is the model family lifestyle and pattern?

Is culture a significant aspect of life?

Use the back of the sheet for other comments.

*Used by permission from Don Umlah.

EXHIBIT 6
Statistical Information

Look for information that includes:

Population of community _____

_____

Housing information: owning or renting, single family homes, apartments, etc. _____

_____

Median income and age of population _____

_____

Ethnic makeup _____

_____

Type of employment and breakdown according to sex _____

_____

Religious preferences _____

_____

Problems facing the community _____

_____

EXHIBIT 7
Analyzing the Statistical Data

To be able to use this information to advantage it will be necessary to ask several questions of it.

1. How has the population change or lack of change been reflected in the membership of the church? _____

_____

_____

_____

2. What kind of a future should we prepare for in regard to our ministry in this community? _____

_____

_____

3. What groups of people do we seem to be unable to reach? _____

_____

_____

_____

4. What are some specific needs of people reflected in that data? _____

_____

_____

_____

5. How are those needs being met at present and by whom? _____

_____

_____

_____

6. What needs should we as a church be addressing? _____

_____

_____

_____

EXHIBIT 8
History of the Community

Here are some suggestions for your community history.

1. Who were the settlers or later immigrants?

   Update—Add current population information.

2. What has been the growth pattern of the community?

   Update—Are there projections for future growth?

3. How was the community organized politically?

   Update—What is the current political structure?
   Is the leadership representative of the entire community or dominated by one part of it?

4. What business or industry first developed in the community?

   Update—What keeps the economy running?
   How is it serviced for food, clothing, housing and furniture, utilities, banking, transportation, businesses and industry?

5. How have the housing patterns developed over the years?

   Update—Current housing information.

6. When did doctors and hospitals begin to practice?

   Update—What recent information regarding health care is available? Is it improving or declining? Is there specialized care offered for the handicapped, the aging, the addicted, and the needy?

7. What was the school system like?

   Update—How has it developed? Are there programs for adults in continuing education? Are there both public and private schools? Do they cooperate with each other?

8. When did any government social service agencies begin?

   Update—Are they still available?

9. What is the history of the police and fire departments?

   Update—How safe do the residents feel in the community? Are certain segments of the population a problem in the community?

10. When did a local newspaper begin publishing?

    Update—Does it still exist? What influence does T.V. or radio have locally?

11. List the growth of churches in the community.

    Update—How many are there today? Do they work together in any manner?

4

Mobilizing for Action

He had been walking all day looking for work or for someone who would help him. He had passed several churches, but he did not stop. He felt he could not take any more rejections. It was getting late in the afternoon, and deep in his guts he was feeling panic.

He and his family had moved to this new city because he thought employment opportunities would be better, but he had not found a job. He began selling their belongings to pay for rent and for food. Everything was gone now except for a little handmade desk that belonged to his little girl, given to her by her grandfather. He could not sell that! Yet he had found no help today, and there was nothing else he could do.

He came to another church. Only the secretary was there. She listened to his story, but she could not authorize church funds. The only money she had was her own. But she said, "Here take some of my money. Let me get you a cup of coffee." He left with an invitation to come back in the morning and talk to one of the pastors.

Someone had actually listened to him. Someone cared!

This is a true story. It tells how a church in Phoenix, Arizona, was introduced to the plight of the city's homeless. This family was rescued from the streets by action taken first by individual members, and later by the total church family. Members of a church discovered how easy it is for a family to slip into the category of "the homeless." Thus a family in desperate need came to know the power of God's healing as their lives were changed and they found God's love.

As a result of your studies, as you begin identifying with your community, many of your worship services can begin to include litanies or special prayers that reflect your discoveries. Consider the insights of Albert Rasmussen:

> Worship that sensitizes us for social responsibility is not some special kind of worship. It is any true worship that humbles and empowers us, deepening our faith to the point that we dare to act upon it, but preserving within us the humility that senses our limitations and our need for new light in every situation.[44]

Through your prayers you have asked God to reveal persons or concerns to you. As you come back from your experiences of community awareness, God will do just that. God will place a burden of concern upon you and your group.

Such was the experience of a small group of church members who met for several weeks to study the Bible and current social issues. They spent time in personal meditation and prayer, confessing their own sins and their need for divine forgiveness. They felt guilt for sins which previously had been hidden from their view: sins which they had committed by failing to act as individuals and sins which they had inherited as members of the larger community, their country, and their world. Later, as they met to share their insights and feelings, it was obvious that the Bible had become real to them in a new way. Becoming aware of their sins of omission, they realized anew their need for God. They identified more with the sinner and experienced the healing and wholeness that come from renewed fellowship with God. A spirit of joy and holiness seemed to take over as they shared with each other, and later as they shared with the larger church fellowship.

Out of their meditation they became united in a surprising concern. It was for the homeless in their community! Although the homeless were never seen out in the suburbs where the members lived, they were highly visible in the downtown area where the church was located. The members recognized a variety of special needs to be met within the church's immediate neighbor-hood, but their initial concern was especially for the homeless. They began to minister by first educating themselves—who were the homeless, how did they come to be homeless, and what were their real needs?

Another church responded to a God-given concern which their pastor had identified. He believed God was calling the members to witness to their own neighbors, and that the church as a whole must witness within its neighbor-hood. The group accepted this concern and began to become acquainted with the families in that neighborhood. In so doing they found an abundance of needs and challenges, both material and spiritual.

It is easier to begin a project when we see a need. We must approach this need with caution to avoid going off on a quixotic crusade. To keep our balance, we need to review biblical instructions and refresh ourselves concerning the ministry of Jesus. We can also use specific techniques that will help us to look effectively at our neighborhood or community. (Suggestions are given in the Activities for Chapter 4.)

Once we identify a specific concern, we can move from an abstract knowledge of the problem to the process of discovering individuals who need help. For example, the Phoenix group who were sympathetic to the needs of the homeless went out to talk with some of them personally. The group found some folk camped under an overpass in the downtown area. The homeless, the group discovered, came from many walks of life, persons who had slipped so far into poverty that they had no place to live. The church people met a young truck driver and his wife who had lost their rig and thus their livelihood. They discovered that this couple knew nothing about living on the streets. Another family, camped beside them, was trying to teach them how to survive. Meeting people like these made the problem personal to the church group.

While visiting this little community of homeless families, the group watched people from the larger community drive up in cars and throw old clothing out the windows without even slowing down. Many of these items were basically junk that no one wanted. In looking through a box, a little five-year-old boy found some old shoelaces and exclaimed, "Grandma, look, we can save these in case we ever need any shoelaces!" The group asked these two families what they needed most. They replied that their primary need was for a bigger cooking pot so that they could use it to carry water from a spigot a block away and share the cooking. Later, members of the group took them specific supplies which would be most helpful. In these and other tangible ways they were able to express God's love and concern to hungry, tired, lonely, and discouraged individuals.

From such personal experiences, poverty became real to a few individuals. They began to explore methods of bringing this same sense of reality to the rest of their church family. They planned a weekend of sharing through which many more church members became involved in community ministry. They organized a food drive. Members were asked to buy an extra sack of groceries each week for three weeks to be given to food banks in the area. Specific items were requested in order to make up hampers which would feed families of four for one week. On the first Sunday after the appeal was made, church members brought 150 sacks of groceries and placed them around the altar at the communion service. As church families shopped for hungry families, poverty became a reality to them.

Christian community ministry becomes a part of the church's outreach when members begin to see, hear, and touch persons in need. Rasmussen has a chapter entitled, "Steps in Building a Church of Influence."[45] These are the steps he outlines:

- Sensitize
- Organize
- Investigate
- Discuss
- Decide
- Act

These things were exactly what the people of the Phoenix church did. They became *sensitive* to the needs of the community, especially the homeless. They *organized* a small group to *investigate* the needs of the community. They *discussed* the needs with the entire church family. They *decided* what they could do to help. They *acted* by bringing food to those who were in desperate need. The steps they took can be followed by any church group.

Marlene Wilson is the author of a book entitled *How to Mobilize Church Volunteers*. She became involved in her own community after reading an article on poverty, thereby sharing the suffering of a woman who had lived in poverty all her life. Ms. Wilson founded an agency designed to match the needs of individuals to resources within the community. She says: "I now know beyond a shadow of a doubt that we do indeed live in a hurting world. The critical question that faces me, and you, and the whole church is, 'What do we intend to do about it?' "

In the Activities section specific guidance is provided for you as you mobilize to meet discovered community needs.

Activities—
Mobilizing for Community Action

It's time for action. We began our process by studying the biblical basis of a social ministry. Then we looked at some of the problems in our world, first in a broad perspective, then more specifically as they exist in our own community. Now we are ready to enlist church members for ministry focusing on revealed community needs. This step calls for several activities growing out of four objectives:

Objective 1: Discover what facilities and services our community does and does not now provide for meeting the needs we have discovered.

Objective 2: Compile information to assist us in our ministry.

Objective 3: Develop action plans.

Objective 4: Devise a plan for making the needs real to church members and enlisting their support.

Guidelines

If you are working in a group—

Over a period of two to three months, meet regularly to develop a strategy for mobilizing your church for community ministry.

1. Develop a broad picture of the needs in your community.

2. Discover the needs your church is already meeting.

3. Examine present goals of your church as they relate to needs.

4. Enlarge your group to encompass more church members.

5. Present the information regarding your neighborhood or community and its needs to your church congregation.

If you are working as an individual—

Select from these pages such activities as you think you can handle, even if they seem very limited. Continue to share your concerns and efforts with others who will give you encouragement.

OBJECTIVE 1: DISCOVER THE NEEDS IN YOUR COMMUNITY AND THE SERVICES THAT ARE PROVIDED.

Activity 1

Obtain information regarding needs and services that will give you a broad picture of your neighborhood or community.

1. Survey community social service agencies, government human service agencies, private nonprofit agencies and church-related organizations. (See Exhibit 9, "Questions to use with Community Agencies." A helpful resource is *The Church That Cares*, by Kenneth R. Miller and Mary Elizabeth Wilson (Valley Forge: Judson Press, 1985). It provides concrete methods for discovering community needs.

2. Interview persons in your community in positions of authority who work with groups of people such as city officials, school personnel, and other community leaders. (You may already have completed this task in Chapter 3 Activities section using Exhibit 5, "Community Questions," and Exhibit 8, "History of the Community.")

Activity 2

Take a survey of community needs that are being met by your church.

1. Interview your pastor to learn about needs which your church is already meeting. Find out who

60

EXHIBIT 9
Questions to Use with Community Agencies

1. Name of agency.

2. Name of person interviewed.

3. What types of services or help do you give to the people you serve?

4. Who are the specific types of people that you serve in this program?

5. Why did your agency initially decide to offer this service?

6. What services do you see still lacking in order to deal with this problem?

7. Have you ever heard of (name of your own church)?

8. Are there ways our church can help you with this problem?

provides the aid. What does it consist of—financial help, material supplies, child care, counseling, or other kinds of aid? Who can qualify for assistance?

2. Look at the history of your church regarding past community ministry. (This information may have been obtained in Chapter 1, Activity 3.) Examine these experiences to determine what succeeded and what failed. Why were some more successful than others? What strengths and weaknesses of your church do you discern or see from these past experiences?

3. Determine how you can capitalize on the revealed strengths of your church for this project.

Activity 3

Consider the present goals of your church.

If Christian community ministry is going to be a priority activity, it must fit into the broader goals of your church.

1. Interview your pastor and church leaders to identify present church goals.

2. Look for ways Christian community ministry can fit into these established goals.

OBJECTIVE 2: COMPILE INFORMATION FROM COMMUNITY AND CHURCH SURVEYS AND INTERVIEWS.

Activity 1

Determine best way to write up information.

1. Decide how the collected information is going to be put together. The task force may divide into groups of two or three persons to work on one part each, and specific members with appropriate skills may be assigned to write up information. Someone also needs to accept responsibility for typing the report.

2. Analyze the information as a group. You have been praying about the need for community ministry for a long time. Continue to pray for God's guidance and power as you analyze the community needs. Study the work you have done in assessing community needs, to determine which of these needs your church might be able to meet. Consider

especially Activity 2 in Chapter 3, and Activity 2 of Objective 1 in Chapter 4.

From the interviews, what needs are most pressing? Are there needs that no one seems to be addressing? Does one specific need match resources your church has to offer?

Is there a group consensus that points to specific needs that should be addressed first? Look for ways to meet them. Can your church handle these alone, or would they be better handled by assisting a social agency? The important question is how best to help needy persons, not how to promote the church.

OBJECTIVE 3: DEVELOP ACTION PLANS.

In the first three chapters you spent time preparing yourself and learning about your community; now you have arrived at the action stage. Don't stop here! Marlene Wilson, trying to involve church members in community service, says:

> I found two common responses. One was ignorance of the need . . . the other was "ignor-ance" (that's knowing about the needs, but doing nothing that really helps to meet them).
> I found that often this kind of response was not because the people didn't care enough; it was because they simply did not know any other way to respond."[47]

Activity 1

Make plans to present community needs and concerns to your church congregation.

1. Select the church organizations that will receive invitations to your presentation. (In some situations it may be best to make separate presentations to various organizations.)

2. At the presentation describe the opportunity you want them to consider and the need(s) to be met.

3. Distribute your analysis of community needs and encourage the people to study the material. Plan for a second meeting.

OBJECTIVE 4: PLAN FOR BRINGING THE REALITY OF COMMUNITY NEEDS TO THE CONGREGATION.

EXHIBIT 10
Social Concerns Ministry
"Solipsism—Can It Be Cured?"

Friday evening, March 4

6:00 to 7:00 p.m.	Potluck (bring a dish)
7:00 to 7:45 p.m.	Bible Study—Matt. 25:31–46 Dr. Ivan Bell
7:45 to 8:30 p.m.	"Without Food and Shelter—the Homeless in Phoenix"
	Speakers: Patti Phillips, Shadow Rock Congregational
	Dr. Louisa Stark, Phoenix So. Community Mental Health Center
8:30 to 9:00 p.m.	Talkback moderated by Warren Ledbetter, board member, Salvation Army

Saturday morning, March 5

9:15 to 9:30 a.m.	Coffee and bagels
9:30 to 10:00 a.m.	Bible Study—Luke 10:25–37 Rev. Henry Barnwell
10:00 to 10:30 a.m.	"Without Equality—the Black Community in Phoenix"
	Speakers: Lucy Connors Vermel Coleman
10:30 to 11:00 a.m.	Talkback: Dorothy Bloom moderating
11:00 to 11:30 a.m.	Fruit and bread break—ABW
11:30 to 12:00 noon	Bible Study—Luke 4:18–19 Rev. James Oines
12:00 to 12:30 p.m.	"Without a Country—the Refugee" *Speakers:* Wanda Alberts Reinhard Geissler Eddie Valdez
12:30 to 1:00 p.m.	Group participation

Activity 1

Stage an event that will educate additional persons about the needs and draw them into a commitment for service.

1. Make the event spectacular. Involve as many people from your church as possible. Exhibit 10, "Faith in Action," illustrates a two-day seminar used by one church to inform and recruit more church members.

Catalog of Creative Ministries, by Virgil and Lynn Nelson, provides information on community and global concerns, and lists ways to dramatize needs. Three examples follow:

1. A care-and-share table can be set up in a suitable area in the church so that those who have surplus food from gardens or fruit trees can share with persons who need food.[48] An event like this can help your church think creatively of other ways to share.

2. A temporary shelter for runaway children like one in Vallejo, California, can be established in a community that has a number of runaways. This would need to be directed by professionals but could be church supported. You could dramatize this need by showing a film on the runaway problem.

3. A neighborhood improvement project such as that of the Milwaukee Christian Center, provides free home repairs for elderly, disabled, and low-income families. The Center hired young unemployed youths to make the needed repairs.[50] This project could be presented by taking members of your church on a tour of the community to see some homes needing repair, or by developing a slide presentation to show the needs. Persons living in some of the homes could be interviewed.

This particular project has many possibilities. In addition to direct help through repair work, your church could campaign for local or county funds to help fix up houses, or it could pressure landlords to make repairs on rental property.

Assign specific responsibilities to each group member. Some possibilities:

1. Coordinate the event so that it will not conflict with other scheduled activities of the church.

2. Publicize the event.

3. Select speakers and guests, and arrange for invitations to be sent.

4. Prepare for the event by making the physical arrangements.

5. Evaluate the response.

Activity 2

Prepare to establish a program for Christian *community ministry.* (See steps outlined in Chapter 5 Activities.)

5

Ready, Set, Go!— Living as a Servant

[The lawyer] answered, "You shall love the Lord your God with all your heart, and with all your soul, and with all your strength, and with all your mind; and your neighbor as yourself." And [Jesus] said to him, "You have answered right; do this, and you will live" (Luke 10:27–28).

Today we stand in the shoes of this lawyer who tested Jesus with a question. God calls us, revealing through Jesus' life and teachings how we are to live. God has prepared us and we are ready. We poise for the final word in the starter's call, "Ready, set, *go!*"

We observed in Chapter 4 how a local church group can commit itself to a program of Christian social ministry in the community. The next critical step is for this ministry to become a vital part of the total church's ongoing program, backed by the encouragement and financial undergirding of the congregation as a whole.

When we become self-satisfied as Christians, God's message should prick us with feelings of discomfort. Often we allow ourselves to be lulled into inertia, satisfied with past accomplishments and therefore believing we deserve a rest. Such inertia, however, does not refresh; it only leads to spiritual deterioration. A feeling of self-satisfaction could be a warning signal to any Christian.

This book, *Church Doors Open Outward*, began because I experienced discomfort. I felt compelled to become involved in the activities I have written about here. I was not satisfied with my Christian discipleship. I knew I needed to be more aware of persons who might be hurting. God had given me a burden to leave my place of ease and share the pain of those around me. I, and those who joined me, began to see the community with new sensitivity. We began building bridges of hope so that we could share God's love and concern with others, and we have discovered needs that we can meet.

In the preceding chapter we discussed ways of mobilizing the local church to make abstract needs real and personal. There is always the danger, however, that enthusiasm for a cause will burn itself out. Therefore, steps to sustain motivation are necessary for an ongoing program of community ministry. The discomfort which prompted us to action is not enough in itself to keep things moving.

A motivation that will sustain a resolve to be the Spirit of Christ in the community, calls for us to take these steps:

- Set reasonable, small, achievable goals
- Know your strengths and weaknesses
- Use time well
- Develop target dates related to expected results
- Use positive feedback and positive reinforcement coming from experiences that have brought some small successes
- Assure continuing success by breaking tasks down into small steps
- Accept moderate risks so that the project continues to be a challenge
- Establish support systems.[51]

Soon after you have established a program of community ministry, it is good to devise a method for evaluation. Needs change, participants in the program move on, and new people will want to help. Ministry must therefore be flexible. Above all, it must remain open to the leading of God's Spirit, which may call for change from time to time. Constant evaluation is therefore very important.

We need to recognize that change often brings personal pain. When we examined the costs of discipleship in Activity 2 of Chapter 1, we discovered that doing the will of God brought poverty, humiliation, temptations, suffering, and finally death to Jesus. In the book of Acts, we learn that the early followers of Jesus were forced to live in poverty because they followed a new faith. They were humiliated; they suffered beatings and insults. Many died as martyrs for their faith. As followers of Jesus, we, too, must be willing to suffer pain. John Bachman in *Faith that Makes a Difference* has written, "The more deeply we love someone, the more we face the possibility—actually the certainty—of separation and sorrow."[52] With separation and sorrow comes pain. As we learn to express God's love, we open ourselves to pain. As we learn to empathize with others who are suffering, we suffer. As we accept the inconveniences of ministering to others, we experience frustration, fatigue, and discouragement. God has not asked us to go around doing good deeds; God has commanded us to accept a new life–style that includes doing good unto others.

"And let us not grow weary in well-doing, for in due season we shall reap, if we do not lose heart. So then, as we have opportunity, let us do good to all men, and especially to those who are of the household of faith" (Galatians 6:9–10).

Any change of direction within a local church has the potential to cause conflict. Just as an individual must accept the reality of pain when following Jesus, so must a church congregation. You may have already discovered that, as your objectives for community ministry are met, opposition often increases, even within the church family. A church fellowship must be willing to live with this tension. Sometimes the majority cannot agree upon a decision to move into some form of community ministry. Many times the decision can only be reached after much discussion. Even though there are times when church groups have found themselves in a breakup or a church "divorce" we must remember that God has called us to love one another in a special way within the fellowship of believers.

There is one body and one Spirit, just as you were called to the one hope that belongs to your call, one Lord, one faith, one baptism, one God and Father of us all who is above all and through all and in all.

—Ephesians 4:4–6

God has not called us to maintain the status quo at any cost. We must remain alive or we die.

"And to the angel of the church in Sardis write: 'The words of him who has the seven spirits of God and the seven stars.
" 'I know your works; you have the name of being alive, and you are dead.' "

—Revelation 3:1

We remain alive as we mature in our faith. Quoting Bachman, "The lukewarm church forgets that it is a community of servants until events remind us of our purpose."[53] As we move closer to God, we become more aware of God's power and glory. As we acknowledge our salvation from our sins we can accept real humility. "You can be humble only when you are conscious of being great," said E. Stanley Jones.[54] Our greatness is the gift of grace from God. Our willingness to become servants is an expression of gratitude for his gift.

There is a second kind of pain we may have to accept, the pain of being alone. In Chapter 4 we examined ways to increase the number of people interested in community ministry. Perhaps your best efforts have met with resistance, you have failed to recruit others, and you feel very alone and discouraged. As we read accounts of men and women who responded to God throughout biblical history, we find that only sometimes were they successful in leading others in new ministries. Often they failed, just as we sometimes fail. What can we do if we find ourselves alone after we have tried to get others to respond to our call to ministry?

Recently I met Celeste, who taught me how God can use one person to accomplish God's will. A young married woman with small children, she lived near a state prison for women. God placed a burden on her heart for the inmates of that prison, and she prayed for them daily for one year. Then God led her to three people—the prison chaplain and two local women with the same concern for the inmates. The three laywomen began to hold a weekly Bible study at the prison. The chaplain taught them how to relate to the prisoners and to discover their real concerns. For two years they ministered in the prison. Then Celeste and her family moved to another city.

Again God called her to resume her work in a women's prison. This time she was all alone. She was not able to find anyone to join her, but she began to visit the prison anyway, where she met the chaplain and obtained permission to hold Bible studies. Finally she was able to recruit a seventy-year-old woman to go with her. But she was not asked to speak about her prison work to any of the groups in the church she had joined. No one seemed interested. A few years passed before she was able to meet with the missions committee of the church. She explained to them that she was not going to the prison on her own, but that, in a sense, she was representing them. The committee then voted to support her by giving her twenty-five dollars with which to buy Bibles and stationery for the women.

When I met Celeste, she had been visiting that prison every week for seven years! She was excited because the Lord was being glorified. Doctors, psychiatric social workers, guards, and administration personnel all responded to her and were opening more doors for her ministry. The women in the prison respected her and were willing to trust her, to listen to her testimony, and to find God themselves. She told me that she had overcome her anger and her pain of working alone. I found her to be a glowing, vibrantly alive woman who had learned to minister with boldness and confidence to the glory of God.

How has her church responded during these seven years? She still receives twenty-five dollars a month for Bibles and stationery, but no one has come forward to visit the prison with her. When a prisoner is released and wants to find a church home, Celeste takes her to a church where she believes the woman will be welcomed. She does not take the woman to her own church because she does not believe the members as a whole have learned how to welcome such women and minister to their needs.

If you find yourself unable to enlist others within your church group to participate with you in discovering God's ministry to others outside the church, follow Celeste's example: Pray for God's direction; look outside your own church fellowship, perhaps to the wider church family, for support; and work alone if necessary.

Celeste taught me another lesson. She said that God really was able to work through her because she had stuck it out for seven years. She said, "No one expected me to keep at it longer than two years at the most." Many times Christians begin to minister in difficult situations but give up too soon. In order to minister effectively to our community we need a sense of God's call, compassion for others, and patience and persistence to stick with the God-appointed task. 2 Peter 1:5–7 suggests attributes we need to pursue:

> For this very reason make every effort to supplement your faith with virtue, and virtue with knowledge, and knowledge with self–control, and self–control with steadfastness, and steadfastness with godliness, and godliness with brotherly affection, and brotherly affection with love.

As we contemplate establishing a program of community ministry in the local church, we must begin by remembering that God wants us to minister to the total person. John Stott suggests how we can do this:

> A human being might be defined from a biblical perspective as 'a body–soul–in community.' That is how God has made us. So if we truly love our neighbours, and because of their worth desire to serve them, we shall be concerned for their total welfare, the well-being of their soul, body, and community. And our concern will lead to practical programmes of evangelism, relief, and development.

Stott believes that the local church's leadership should encourage persons with identical concerns to form "special interest groups" or "study with action groups." He cites several examples:

> Some will have an evangelistic objective—house-to-house visitation, a music group, a world mission group, etc. Other groups will have a social concern— sick and welfare visitors, a housing association, community or race relations,

. . . the needs of an ethnic minority, etc. Such specialist groups supplement one another.

This guidebook has been written to help you form a study and action group. Now you should be ready to establish community ministry as a part of your church's long-range objectives.

As your church readies for this task, community ministry will no longer be an occasional "baskets-at-Thanksgiving-and-Christmas" response, but a major program. You will discover the satisfaction and joy that come from being the presence of the caring Christ to your neighborhood.

Activities—
"Ready, Set, Go!"

Here you are given a step-by-step action plan for moving out into meaningful community ministry. You also face the question, "What if my church is not yet ready to undertake such a program?"

The suggested activities are grouped under two objectives:

Objective 1: Develop a program of community ministry.

Objective 2: Choose optional plans if necessary.

Guidelines

If you are working in a group—

1. Set goals and objectives for a continuing program of community ministry.

2. Develop action plans.

3. Bring action plans to the pastor and governing board.

4. Arrange for a permanent committee or coordinator to administer a program of community ministry.

5. Begin with one program.

6. Evaluate the program regularly.

7. Consider options.

If you are working as an individual—

Follow the example of Celeste in Chapter 5. Pray for God's guidance and strength. Look beyond your own church—to the wider church fellowship or to the community—for support, and be willing to work alone if necessary.

OBJECTIVE 1: DEVELOP A PROGRAM OF COMMUNITY MINISTRY.

Activity 1:

Set goals and objectives for the program.

1. Enlarge your task force, drawing upon individuals and groups you have recruited as a result of Chapter 4 Activities.

The book *How to Mobilize Church Volunteers,* by Marlene Wilson, can be helpful. The author lists the following reasons why people volunteer:

- They want to be needed.
- They want to help others and make a difference.
- They want to learn new skills or use skills they already have.
- They want to belong to a caring community and feel accepted as members.
- They want self-esteem and affirmation.
- They want to grow in their faith and share their God-given gifts.
- They want to keep from being lonely.
- They want to support causes they believe in."[57]

2. List suggested goals and objectives for a program of community ministry. To do so, form several small groups to do some brainstorming. Then reconvene to share the results of brainstorming and select goals and objectives.

3. Write out a mission statement so that church members will understand what you wish to accomplish. Be specific. Your purpose is to help many people understand how they can fit into such a ministry. Some may want to be heavily involved, others may want to contribute a smaller amount of time and effort.

Activity 2:

Develop action plans.

1. Determine how you wish your church to proceed.

2. Select several optional community needs to present to the church.

3. Describe the need and action your group recommends.

4. Develop a survey form for use by the church's governing board or the congregation (see Exhibit 11, "Christian Community Ministry Questionnaire"). Ask them to select the need they believe is most important and to tell you how they could help to meet that need.

Activity 3

Bring goals, objectives, and action plans to the proper decision-making body.

1. Allow sufficient time for church leaders to become thoroughly acquainted with the information you are presenting. A retreat is an excellent way to provide the time and to establish a sense of purpose.

2. Explain seven steps necessary to sustain a program:
- Set reasonable goals.
- Know your own strengths and weaknesses. (Distribute material developed on the church's strengths and weaknesses.)
- Use time well.
- Develop target dates for expected results.
- Use feedback.
- Accept moderate risks.
- Establish a support system.

3. Give examples of how a church can establish a program of community ministry. One source is the book *Effective Urban Church Ministry*, by G. Willis Bennett (Nashville: Broadman Press, 1983). Another source is Exhibit 12, "Church of the Redeemer Develops a Program for Community Ministry."

Activity 4

Decide on a need that the church will begin to address. Begin with one program and add others as the Holy Spirit leads.

1. Select a permanent committee to work on setting in motion action plans developed by the task force. You may use a committee that already exists or form a new one. One church organized a committee for local and church social needs which they called "The Samaritan Committee."

2. Choose one person to assume leadership for the program. This could be a volunteer coordinator of community ministry, or the church may wish to employ someone for this purpose. Having a coordinator provides stability and a sense of permanence to the ministry. The coordinator screens volunteers and helps match them to their tasks.

Activity 5

Evaluate the program at least annually.

1. Make a yearly written evaluation of who was served and how. (You could make this report more often, if desirable, to encourage volunteers and those supporting the program.)

2. Continue to update your knowledge of community organizations, including how you can assist each other and what needs are not being met.

OBJECTIVE 2: PREPARE BACKUP PLANS.

Activity 1

Consider alternative approaches for church support.

1. Step back and wait. Then evaluate any resistance to community ministry.

2. Decide on a course of action. When a great deal of tension threatens the effectiveness of the ministry of your church, you must be willing to move back from conflict and pray for guidance. There are many books dealing with the subject of conflict within the church. Chapter 4 of *The Church That Cares*, by Kenneth R. Miller and Mary Elizabeth Wilson (Valley Forge: Judson Press, 1985) is devoted to the subject. Follow the guidelines for conflict management suggested.

Activity 2

Work with other groups within the community to do community ministry.

1. Become a volunteer with one or more existing agencies or church organizations that might be friendly to your project.

2. Enlist others outside the church to organize a response to your project.

Activity 3

Work alone if necessary.

Realize that any of us can become aware of a hurting world. We can examine ourselves and our own gifts for ministry.

And his gifts were that some should be apostles, some prophets, some evangelists, some pastors and teachers, to equip the saints for the work of ministry, for building up the body of Christ.

—Ephesians 4:11–12

Activity 4

Commit yourself to becoming a servant of God.

As we serve we discover the truth of the Scripture: "And my God will supply every need of yours according to his riches in glory in Christ Jesus. To our God and Father be glory for ever and ever. Amen" (Philippians 4:19–20).

EXHIBIT 11
Christian Community Ministry Questionnaire

Explain work of task force and identified needs.

List first need _____
Write out your recommendation for ministry and explain.

(　) I will personally support this recommendation.

(　) I think the church should be involved with this ministry.

(　) I do not support this recommendation.

Comments: _____

List second need _____
Write out your recommendation for ministry and explain.

(　) I will personally support this recommendation.

(　) I think the church should be involved with this ministry.

(　) I do not support this recommendation.

Comments: _____

Name _____
(We would appreciate your signing this
questionnaire, although this is optional.)

EXHIBIT 12
Church of the Redeemer Develops
a Program for Community Ministry

In 1983, Church of the Redeemer in Mesa, Arizona, developed service groups for key areas of ministry for congregational involvement. The goals for the laity were:

(1) One deacon was assigned to each key ministry.

(2) Service groups were formed with a qualified person within the group selected to assume the responsibility of coordinator. The deacon acted as liaison between the group and the church leadership.

(3) Each group decided how often it would meet to set goals, discuss needs, and take action.

The areas of ministry were determined by a commitment sheet that listed a number of selected possibilities developed by the pastor and the deacons. Each member was given opportunity to select an area of ministry. Some of the programs ministered to persons in need within the church and others to persons in the community. Some outreach was to be carried out in cooperation with other community agencies and some by the church members themselves.

I interviewed one of the pastors to discuss the history of his involvement in community ministry. Here is his story:

When he came to the church several years earlier, there was no social concerns program for local outreach. He was challenged to become involved in the problems of the world by a lay couple in the church. The pastor said that his first steps in awareness had begun five or six years earlier when he read a number of books on social concern and social action. He often preached on these subjects, but it seemed no one was listening. Through this lay couple he now was being urged to become personally involved.

Finally, he accepted their challenge for personal involvement. He became a member of a Foster Care Review Board, a community-based board to review and advise action on all local foster-care cases involving the state. As a board member and later as chairman of the board, he succeeded in bringing a Christian perspective to this secular organization. He also developed a deep concern for children who had been abused or neglected. He and his wife decided to become foster parents. He worked with two nonprofit Christian organizations; one was an adoption and foster care agency and the other a pregnancy crisis center.

As they became personally involved, the members of his church began to hear what he was preaching. They began to follow his example. He said, "Actions follow belief." The members began to live out their real theology, which included community ministry. The pastor believes that ministers must encourage members in three ways. "First, by using the pulpit to instruct biblical truths on 'bearing one another's burdens' and to increase the congregation's awareness of community needs. Second, the pastor shares little by little his or her concerns and theology through personal contacts. He or she encourages members on a one-to-one basis to use their particular spiritual gifts. Third, the pastor models the actions he or she is requesting of the members."

Let us go back and put this story into the seven steps for sustaining a program.

1. *Set reasonable goals.* Reasonable goals were set for the church leadership and for members.
2. *Know your strengths and weaknesses.* Members were asked to evaluate their spiritual gifts before signing up for action.
3. *Use time well.* Each group organized independently so that it could use its time as needed.
4. *Develop target dates and set consequences.* Organization helped each group to meet this step by having a coordinator who was responsible to the group for their specific area of ministry. A deacon who acted as liaison between the group and church leadership helped to keep the group on target. The pastor also accepted responsibility to become involved personally with the groups.
5. *Use feedback.* Positive feedback came from the pulpit where official recognition was made of the services being given. The pastor continued to provide biblical instruction and awareness of community concerns.
6. *Accept moderate risks.* The church leadership began to discuss risky subjects regarding social issues, to study Scriptures to see what action God commanded, to pray and meditate on the social issues, and then to develop statements of concern that committed the church to an open stand on a particular issue.
7. *Establish support systems.* Since groups were composed of people with like interests, they served as a support system for each other. The church had deliberately chosen to support the group system by giving it official church recognition as an important part of the church program structure.

The Church of the Redeemer called these programs the Diaconal Ministries (the work of servantship). It used 1 Timothy 3:13 as the biblical basis: "For those who serve well as deacons gain a good standing for themselves and also great confidence in the faith which is in Christ Jesus."

Notes

[1]William Barclay, *And He Had Compassion* (Valley Forge: Judson Press, 1976), p. 3.

Chapter 1

[2]For these ideas I am indebted to Gosta Lundstrom, *The Kingdom of God in the Teaching of Jesus* (Richmond: John Knox Press, 1963).

[3]*Ibid.*

[4]David O. Moberg, *Inasmuch: Christian Social Responsibility in the Twentieth Century* (Grand Rapids: William B. Eerdmans Publishing Company, 1965), p. 18.

[5]*Ibid.*, p. 17.

[6]Ron Haskins and James J. Gallagher, eds., *Models for Analysis of Social Policy: An Introduction* (Norwood, N.J.: Ablex Publishing Corporation, 1981), pp. 86–87.

[7]Albert Terrill Rasmussen, *Christian Social Ethics* (Englewood Cliffs: Prentice-Hall, Inc., 1956), p. 63.

[8]Bruce C. Birch and Larry L. Rasmussen, *The Predicament of the Prosperous* (Philadelphia: The Westminster Press, 1978), p. 47.

[9]Moberg, *op. cit.*, p. 31.

[10]*Ibid.*, p. 32.

[11]Esther Byle Bruland and Stephen Charles Mott, *A Passion for Jesus; A Passion for Justice* (Valley Forge: Judson Press, 1983), p. 35.

[12]William Barclay, *Jesus as They Saw Him* (New York: Harper & Row, Publishers, Inc., 1962), p. 186.

[13]Hillyer Hawthorne Straton, *A Guide to the Parables of Jesus* (Grand Rapids: Wm. B. Eerdmans Publishing Company, 1959), p. 110.

[14]*Ibid.*, p. 111.

[15]*Ibid.*, p. 112.

[16]*Ibid.*, p. 113.

[17]*Ibid.*, p. 114.

[18]*Ibid.*, p. 115.

[19]Bruland and Mott, *op. cit.*, p. 35.

[20]Robert G. Clouse, ed., *Wealth and Poverty: Four Christian Views of Economics* (Downers Grove: Inter-Varsity Press, 1984), p. 20.

Chapter 2

[21]Bruce C. Birch and Larry L. Rasmussen, *op. cit.*, p. 53.

[22]Women's Work Force, a project of Wider Opportunities for Women, Inc., *The Feminization of Poverty* (Charleston, W. Va.: Women & Employment, Inc., 1918).

[23]Martin Luther King, Jr., *Letter from a Birmingham Jail* (Valley Forge: American Baptist Churches in the U.S.A.), p. 10.

[24]Native American Consulting Committee, Presbyterian Church U.S.A., *A Strategy to Build a Native American Endowment for Leadership Development.*

[25]*Nutrition Week*, August 9, 1984, p. 8.

[26]*Ibid.*

[27]*A Policy Framework for Racial Justice*, with a foreword by Kenneth B. Clark and John Hope Franklin (Washington: Joint Center for Political Studies, 1983), p. ix.

[28]Stephen Glenn and Joel W. Warner, *Developing Capable Young People* (Hurst, Texas: Humansphere, Inc., 1982). Quotation taken from tape of a lecture by H. Stephen Glenn.

[29]"The Changing Face of America," *Time*, July 8, 1985, p. 29.

[30]*Ibid.*, pp. 27–28.

[31]*Ibid.*, p. 27.

[32]"A Most Debated Issue," *Time*, July 8, 1985, p. 75.

[33]"John W. Bachman, *Faith That Makes a Difference* (Minneapolis: Augsburg Publishing House, 1983), p. 28.

[34]Orlando E. Costas, "The Hispanics Next Door," *The Christian Century*, August 18–25, 1982, pp. 851–852.

[35]Native American Consulting Committee, *op. cit.*, p. 7.

[36]Vine Deloria, Jr., *God Is Red* (New York: Dell Publishing Co., Inc., 1973), p. 38.
[37]R. Pierce Beaver, *Introduction to Native American Church History* (Tempe, Ariz.: Cook Christian Training School, 1983), p. 192.

Chapter 3

[38]Linnea O. Foss, *Turn to Me and Live* (Berkeley: American Baptist Seminary of the West, 1983), p. 55.
[39]Bachman, *op. cit.*, p. 21.
[40]Duncan McIntosh and Richard Rusbuldt, *Planning Growth in Your Church* (Valley Forge: Judson Press, 1983), p. 25.
[41]*Ibid.*, p. 142.
[42]Richard E. Rusbuldt, Richard K. Gladden, Norman M. Green, Jr., *Local Church Planning Manual* (Valley Forge: Judson Press, 1977).
[43]*Ibid.*

Chapter 4

[44]Rasmussen, *op. cit.*, p. 178.
[45]*Ibid.*, pp. 175ff.
[46]Marlene Wilson, *How to Mobilize Church Volunteers* (Minneapolis: Augsburg Publishing House, 1983), p. 104.
[47]*Ibid.*, p. 107.
[48]Virgil and Lynn Nelson, *Catalog of Creative Ministries: Over 300 Ideas That Work* (Valley Forge: Judson Press, 1983), p. 80.
[49]*Ibid.*, p. 62.
[50]*Ibid.*, p. 83.

Chapter 5

[51]I am grateful to Dr. Robert Scott, of the Department of Behavioral Sciences, Pennsylvania State University, for the use of material on which these steps are based.
[52]Bachman, *op. cit.*, p. 107.
[53]*Ibid.*, p. 88.
[54]E. Stanley Jones, *In Christ* (Nashville: Abingdon Press, 1980), p. 95.
[55]John Stott, *Involvement: Being a Responsible Christian in a Non-Christian Society* (Old Tappan: Fleming H. Revell Company, 1985), p. 41.
[56]*Ibid.*, p. 51.
[57]Wilson, *op. cit.*, p. 87.